NOSH

VEGAN PLANT-BASED & DOWN-TO-EARTH

BY JOY MAY

THE NOSH SERIES OF COOKBOOKS BY JOY MAY

NOSH VEGAN PLANT-BASED & DOWN-TO-EARTH — JOY MAY
ISBN: 9780993260971

NOSH EVERYDAY GLUTEN-FREE — DELICIOUS, GO-TO-RECIPES FOR EVERY DAY OF THE WEEK — JOY MAY
ISBN: 9780993260964

NOSH GLUTEN-FREE — A NO-FUSS, EVERYDAY GLUTEN-FREE COOKBOOK FROM THE NOSH FAMILY — JOY MAY
ISBN: 9780956746450

NOSH GLUTEN-FREE BAKING — A NO-FUSS, GLUTEN-FREE COOKBOOK FROM THE NOSH FAMILY — JOY MAY
ISBN: 9780956746498

NOSH SUGAR-FREE GLUTEN-FREE — SAYING 'NO' TO PROCESSED SUGAR AND GLUTEN NEVER TASTED SO GOOD — JOY MAY
ISBN: 9780993260919

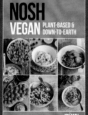

NOSH QUICK & EASY — JOY MAY
ISBN: 9780956746481

NOSH FOR STUDENTS — 5TH EDITION PHOTO WITH EVERY RECIPE — A FUN STUDENT COOKBOOK — OVER 200,000 STUDENT NOSH BOOKS SOLD — JOY MAY
ISBN: 9780993260933

VEGETARIAN **NOSH** FOR STUDENTS — 3RD EDITION PHOTO WITH EVERY RECIPE — A FUN STUDENT COOKBOOK — OVER 200,000 STUDENT NOSH BOOKS SOLD — JOY MAY
ISBN: 9780993260940

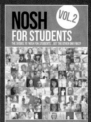

NOSH FOR STUDENTS VOL.2 — THE SEQUEL TO NOSH FOR STUDENTS ...GET THE OTHER ONE FIRST! — OVER 200,000 STUDENT NOSH BOOKS SOLD — JOY MAY
ISBN: 9780956746467

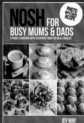

NOSH FOR BUSY MUMS & DADS — PHOTO WITH EVERY RECIPE — A FAMILY COOKBOOK WITH EVERYDAY FOODS FOR REAL FAMILIES — JOY MAY
ISBN: 9780993260957

  } @NOSHBOOKS

CONTENTS

This book has been a long time in the making! I have been writing cookbooks with my family for about 18 years now and have lost count of the times we have been asked to write a vegan book. My ethos over the years has always been to provide recipes which are simple, straightforward and accessible for everyday meals, and are written in such a way as to make them eminently achievable as well as tasty.

I am what I would call a 'down-to-earth foodie', passionate about food, but without the pretension that can sometimes come with it. I don't write books to impress people I write them to be used by people.

I love getting people to eat healthy and delicious food, and also helping people who have specific food needs and passions to achieve a healthy and nutritious diet. My first book, 'NOSH for Students', was written for my son Ben, and was aimed at encouraging and enabling students to eat healthier where the obvious, and often reached for alternative, was a ready-made meal or takeaway.

In more recent years, we have concentrated on serving the 'free-from' world by aiming to take the mystery out of, what may seem at first glance, a restrictive diet.

We have approached the vegan, or 'plant-based' world, in a similar way (although in some different ways, as I will explain later) creating accessible, achievable, simple, delicious recipes, that use wonderful, fresh ingredients. Hopefully, this will avoid the need to buy prepackaged foods such as sausages, burgers and meat-substitute foods that come with their inevitable preservative-laden issues.

Vegan cookery is a potential 'hotbed' for creativity; we loved being taken along with it. We very much enjoyed playing with ingredients that we had never even touched before, or had at least, totally forgotten about.

We aimed to use fresh ingredients as much as possible, although, inevitably, some things used were in tins, for example, lentils, so that we could reduce the cooking times.

One of the biggest surprises throughout the writing of this book has been how it has affected my approach to food in general. It has caused a realignment of how I write recipes; not being reliant on single key ingredients, but often focusing more on multiple elements that add up to make a greater 'whole'. Perhaps no other book I have written has challenged my approach as much as this one. Our plates have never been so colourful!!!

WHO IS THIS BOOK FOR?

It might seem fairly obvious who this book is aimed at, but, to give you an insight into how our minds work here at NOSH, we thought we would clarify this.

BEGINNERS We have tried to make this book as 'accessible' as possible; those just entering the world of veganism, or plant-based diets, are very much on our minds. You may be totally clueless as to where to start, so we hope this book goes some way to holding your hand through those early stages. We want to introduce you gradually to some new ingredients and even give you some tips on where to find them in the supermarkets.

OLD-TIMERS We are fully aware that you could probably tell us a thing or two about vegan cooking, but you might still be looking for some inspiration when you have got into a rut, cooking those old 'classics' a little too often. We really hope that we have written a book that gives you some inspiration.

TOE-DIPPERS You might not yet be fully signed up to the concept of a plant-based diet, or you could have just heard it on the news and wondered what everyone was talking about. We are here to show you that you can get delicious meals from plants alone, plants packed with colour and flavour. Whether you end up being a full 'convert' or not, we hope that at least you will be able to appreciate that there is a whole world of flavours just waiting for you to try.

THIS IS OUR MUG

Since our first-ever book, 'NOSH for Students', we have included a method of measuring ingredients, using the common mug, in almost every book we have written. The idea behind it is that things can be as simple as grabbing a mug and getting started. Cooking isn't always about perfection, it is about getting food on the table, food full of flavour, with as few obstacles as possible. If you prefer to use weighing scales, we won't be offended (and we have included the grams and ml measures too), but we are just giving you the option to get cooking straight away.

The mug here is 'life-size' and measures ½ a pint (about 300ml). Choose a mug which is close to this in volume and you won't go wrong.

ACTUAL SIZE

10 THINGS THAT ARE (MAYBE) SURPRISINGLY NOT VEGAN

If you are used to 'shopping vegan' you will know it is relatively simple and straightforward. As long as you keep alert and read the ingredient labels carefully, you should be fine. I find that shopping online makes things very easy, as most of the supermarket sites state clearly what is and what is not 'vegan'.

However, you would think that with today's technological advancements we wouldn't need to use animal products in the actual production-process of our food, but it still manages to creep in somehow. We have pulled together some of the most surprising foodstuffs that might contain animal products that you need to watch out for.

1 DAIRY-FREE PRODUCTS – ER...MEAT

This one could seem like a no-brainer, but we still need to apply common sense. Just because it has got the dairy-free stamp, it may still contain other animal products. A beef steak is dairy-free, so is chicken, but they are certainly not vegan. We need to make sure it is vegan friendly too!

2 PESTO – ANIMAL RENNET

'Normal' pesto is not only unsuitable for vegans it is also unsuitable for vegetarians, as traditional Parmesan is made with animal rennet. You can just search for vegan-friendly stuff or, even better, make your own. We have got a quick recipe on page 66.

3 HONEY – DEAD BEES

This one can be a debatable issue. The process of producing much of our honey can either harm bees by taking food sources from them, or even destroy them altogether. Therefore, we have avoided using honey.

4 BEER AND WINE – FISH BLADDER

Ever looked at the label on wine or beer and seen that it contains milk, or even fish? Not quite what you expect when you are tucking into a crisp and fruity Pinot Grigio, or supping a nice 'hoppy' ale. Nevertheless, part of the filtration process can involve these products, so you need to do your research. All is not lost; you can still have your chosen 'tipple', you just have to work a little harder to find it.

5 WHITE SUGAR – ANIMAL BONES

This one has some really big implications when it comes to narrowing our choice of vegan-friendly food. Those pearly white granules didn't start out like that and, apparently, a common way of getting it to look like that is to use 'bone char'. Don't be fooled by its more natural-looking cousin, brown sugar, as, invariably, it has been through the same weird process and then had molasses added to it, to give it that 'authentic look'. If you can't quit the white stuff, all is not lost, there are still brands out there which filter without using animal products. Again, you just need to read the labels.

6 ORANGE JUICE – FISH OIL AND LANOLIN

We thought orange juice was good enough on its own! Apparently, some manufacturers think it needs fortifying with Omega 3 from fish oil and Vitamin D, in the form of lanolin from sheep's wool. A lot of juice is totally fine, but again, look out for anything that says it is 'fortified'.

7 ENHANCED BREADS – FISH OIL

In a similar way to the additives in orange juice, bread can get the same treatment. Bread is something you need to look at anyway, as it can easily contain your more obvious non-vegan ingredients, such as honey, eggs, whey, milk and butter.

8 MARGARINE – WHEY AND GELATIN

This is similar to the 'dairy-free products' mentioned above. Just because it's made with various oils, rather than butter, it can still have some lurking 'baddies' included, such as gelatine and casein (derived from milk). A note on casein: (you can do your own research on it, because it is super-geeky) it is used in the production of glue for fireproof doors. I don't know about you, but I don't really fancy that in my food.

9 PACKAGED PEANUTS – GELATIN

We already know not to eat nuts that are put out on the counters in pubs and bars (if you don't know what I am talking about, just 'Google' it and you will see it is not nice!), but we also need to be more careful and make sure the nuts we use are not produced using gelatine. I have no idea why you would need to add gelatine to the simple nut, but there you go.

10 SOY-BASED YOGURTS & CHEESES – CASEIN

"Please, say it isn't true! Don't take soy away from us!!" Don't panic, there is nothing wrong with soy itself, but, just because it is a soy product, it doesn't mean it is vegan. That pesky casein can rear its ugly head in some of these products, so we just need to check the labels again. Do you think I have said the phrase 'check the label' too many times?

FOR WHAT IT IS WORTH, THIS IS WHAT WE THINK ABOUT NUTRITION

DISCLAIMER ALERT!! We are not nutritionists, or doctors, we just love food and want to help people to be healthy. Anything we say in this book is our 'take' on all of the research we have read out there. If we say something you think is crazy, why not get in touch on our Facebook page (@noshbooks) and we can chat. Maybe we are missing something.

It is pretty well-documented that a vegan diet helps prevent all sorts of illnesses: diabetes, heart disease, strokes, cancer and Alzheimer's, to name just a few. Great news, right? Well, not so fast. We can't just switch off and relax believing that a vegan diet is guaranteed to be 'healthy'. As with any diet, if we don't plan what we eat, we can miss out on some of the major nutrients our bodies need.

You will see on the following pages that we have included a chart at the bottom of each recipe to help you understand its nutritional components. In particular, we show the recommended daily allowance (RDA) against each element and how it contributes overall in that recipe. We understand, however, that you may have nutritional requirements which are different to the recommended levels, that depend on your own personal, health goals.

The chart does not include the vitamins and minerals necessary for a balanced diet, so we have attempted to highlight throughout the book some of the key ones, and also those less easy to access. For example, vitamin B12, which is not present in plant foods, can be introduced via the intake of nutritional yeast, sushi nori seaweed, and fortified soy products.

WILL THIS BOOK BE GOOD FOR ME?

Right then…cards on the table. This could be a terrible idea, as we have never seen any other cookbook giving this information out so openly.

We want to show you what your health would look like if you cooked using our book for all your meals. Is our book for you? Let's see!

We have taken the average for each of our breakfasts, lunches and dinners and added them together to make a full day of eating. Below is the average nutrition you will get from meals across the whole of the book.

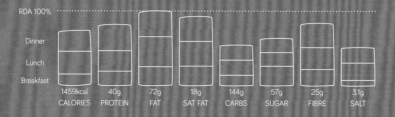

So what do we see from our graphs? Well, there are some things that are easy to comment on, so let's pick them out first to get us going.

SALT

Our salt content is well below the recommended limit at 52% of RDA, because on the whole, we are deciding what salt to add as an ingredient, rather than it being 'pre-packaged' in the ingredients themselves. When adding salt to a meal, we would always recommend freshly ground, high quality, sea salt, as opposed to normal table salt, that is so refined that it has lost most of its valuable minerals.

FIBRE

Most people in the UK only get just over half of the fibre they need in their daily diet. With this book you will get 84% of RDA. The benefits of fibre are numerous, including helping to maintain a healthy weight, and lowering the risk of diabetes, heart disease and some cancers.

PROTEIN

We are very pleased to see that protein has come out well at 80% of RDA. If you are exercising lots, and want to boost your protein intake, why not 'top up', every now and then, with something like our energy bars on p190 and p188. We go into more detail on protein in the next couple of pages, so have a look there if you are interested.

CARBS & SUGAR

The carb and sugar levels are interesting too. At 56% and 63%, respectively, they are well within your RDA, so if trimming your weight, or keeping it at a 'good level', is one of your priorities, then these stats will definitely support this. Even the sugar content is mainly made up from non-processed, natural sugars, meaning that they will release slowly into the blood, avoiding the unhealthy sugar-spikes found in the refined 'white stuff'. We go into more detail on sugar later in the book.

FATS

You can see from the fat and saturated fat content-levels that we are right at the upper limit of our RDA's, at 102% and 90% respectively.

For some this might be of concern, but the make-up of the fat is probably the more important aspect to examine. A great deal of the fat comes from nuts, such as Brazils, peanuts and cashews, from avocados and coconut milk, and from natural oils used for frying, such as olive oil, coconut oil and rapeseed oil. Fat is no longer seen as the 'Public Enemy #1' it once was. Fat is important for a healthy diet and has the benefit of reducing sugar cravings, but it is still important to get our fats from good, natural sources. When it comes to oils used for frying we recommend oils with the minimum of processing and in their 'virgin state' wherever possible. We have introduced rapeseed oil into this book; it has the lowest saturated fat content of any cooking oil, is a great source of Omega 3 oils and also boasts a high smoke point. Increasingly it is being used by chefs from around the world. We would most definitely recommend using 'virgin, cold-pressed rapeseed oil'.

CALORIES

Now, to calories, which, at 73% of RDA, is an interesting 'component'. Keeping your eating at this level, without additional food intake, would definitely be classed as being low in calories and thus assist weight loss. Some of us will want to load up on more calories as fuel for exercise, or muscle-gain. If you want more calories, then you can always increase your portion sizes by adding extra rice, pasta or potatoes. From a calorific point of view, you could even afford to have a dessert each day, but we are going to leave this one up to you.

So there we go, our cards on the table. No hiding. If you are still reading this, then you can't have thrown the book away in disgust and run out of the bookshop. We are just presenting what we have done. We are not doctors, and you can make up your mind as to what you think and what your goals are. Hopefully all this is helpful to you.

PROTEIN, PROTEIN, PROTEIN

"...but where will you get your protein from?"

I am pretty sure you will have heard this before, as it is often one of the first things sceptics will come at you with when you tell them you are 'meat and dairy-free'. We couldn't write a plant-based book and not talk about the sticky issue of protein. So let's give it a go.

There is no doubt that you could more easily load up with protein on a meat, or animal product-based diet, but it is also well achievable within a plant-based diet. As long as you know what to look out for, and know a couple of important things about how protein works, you should be fine.

With protein, the issue is not about getting enough, it is about getting 'the right mix'. Not all protein is created equal, or 'complete'. The concept of being 'complete' is all about amino acids, the building blocks of protein. We need 20 different types of amino acids in our body. Thankfully our bodies give us a head start by producing 11 of those 20. So we only need to consume the remaining 9, in roughly equal amounts, for us to achieve our complete, essential amino acids.

Does it still sound too complicated? Don't worry, it gets simpler. Keep reading.

Whereas meat and dairy products do provide the essential amino acids, there are plant-based ingredients we can easily consume that do just the same. The great thing is, we don't need to worry that every mouthful, or even every meal, contains complete proteins. As long as we eat a variety of protein sources every day, we should be fine.

Soy, quinoa, hempseed and chia all provide complete proteins on their own. The following combinations of food also provide complete proteins:

- Black beans and rice
- Pasta and peas
- Wholewheat bread and peanut butter

- Roasted nuts, seeds together with peanuts
- Hummus (chickpeas and tahini)
- Almonds and lentils

Hopefully, this shows how simple it can be. We believe that one of the keys is not to load up on one type of protein all the time; instead, just mix it up and keep a diet which is full of the wonderful, varied, plant-based products.

WHAT ABOUT SUGAR?

As we have already mentioned, it is not always easy to know whether the sugar you are using is vegan friendly. Some processed sugar manufacturers still use 'bone char' as part of their processing.

Thankfully, Tate and Lyle and Billingtons sugars are vegan friendly. Most Silver Spoon products are suitable for vegans too, apart from the different types of icing sugar and fondant icing products they offer. You also need to be careful with artificial sweeteners, as many of them have been tested on animals. Personally, I would never recommend artificial sweeteners as they can promote an addiction to highly sweet foodstuffs and mess with the tastebuds.

Another big problem caused by the sugar-processing industry is that it strips the sugar of all of its natural nutrients, leaving only pure calories with no benefits, apart from a quick burst of energy that we may never use! In this book we have sought to use the most suitable, natural sugars 'packaged' naturally with vitamins, fibres, antioxidants and minerals. These give us all the amazing health-benefits, together with a slow release of sugar into our systems, rather than the 'sugar-spikes' we get from highly-processed sugars.

In recipes which require sweetness, we have used pure, maple syrup and organic, raw coconut sugar as much as possible.

In the 'sweet' section, there are a few deviations from the above, mainly because ingredients often struggle to hold together when using unrefined sugars. We would consider these as treats and they are not intended to be part of an everyday diet. In these instances you will need to use vegan, white sugar.

WEIRD AND WONDERFUL INGREDIENTS

If you are a seasoned vegan, this may not apply, but below are a few ingredients we use in this book which you may not be familiar with. On the whole, we have tried to use ingredients readily available in most supermarkets.

SUSHI NORI SEAWEED:

The Japanese have been eating this for centuries and they credit it with giving long life. Who could argue with that? A single sheet can give you half of your RDA of B12. Great news!

NUTRITIONAL YEAST

This is an excellent source of vitamin B12, an essential vitamin not found in plant-based foods. It can be bought in flaked form and is easily added to sauces. It gives a bit of a savoury flavour to them.

POMEGRANATE MOLASSES

Gives a wonderful piquant flavour to dishes. It is simply pomegranate juices, heated and reduced down to a thick syrup and still retaining a lot of the goodness.

AGAR FLAKES

Used in desserts, they help to 'set' the ingredients. Used in place of something like gelatine, which is animal-based.

MILLED FLAX SEEDS

Used in order to hold things together in the way that eggs do. You need to soak them in a little water for 10 minutes before using them.

MISO PASTE

Made from soy beans, rice and yeast, it adds a lovely, savoury flavour to oriental dishes.

ACKEE

The national fruit of Jamaica, it is bright yellow and great, scrambled with onions and tomatoes.

JACKFRUIT

The national fruit of Bangladesh and Sri Lanka, jackfruit is great in savoury dishes and, when slow-cooked, pulls apart and absorbs flavour and sauce beautifully.

RAS EL HANOUT

A mix of spices, that originate from North Africa. Often used in tagines.

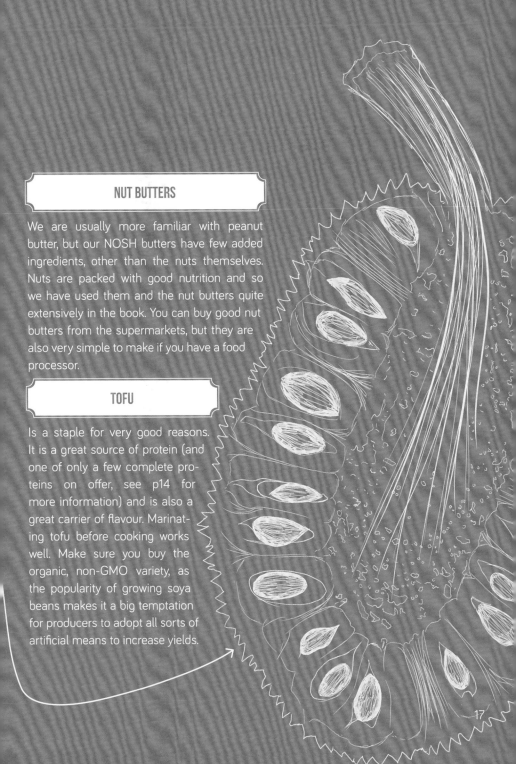

NUT BUTTERS

We are usually more familiar with peanut butter, but our NOSH butters have few added ingredients, other than the nuts themselves. Nuts are packed with good nutrition and so we have used them and the nut butters quite extensively in the book. You can buy good nut butters from the supermarkets, but they are also very simple to make if you have a food processor.

TOFU

Is a staple for very good reasons. It is a great source of protein (and one of only a few complete proteins on offer, see p14 for more information) and is also a great carrier of flavour. Marinating tofu before cooking works well. Make sure you buy the organic, non-GMO variety, as the popularity of growing soya beans makes it a big temptation for producers to adopt all sorts of artificial means to increase yields.

BREAKFAST

QUINOA PANCAKES

Pancakes are often considered a bit of a naughty way to start the day. However, this quinoa variety is great for breakfast as it gives you a nice shot of protein to stave off hunger 'till lunch-time.

1 tablespoon **milled flax seeds**

3 tablespoons **water**

75g **ground almonds**

150g **quinoa flour**

1 teaspoon **baking powder**

1 mug/300ml **soy milk**

4 tablespoons **maple syrup**

1 tablespoon **coconut oil**

150g **blueberries**

150g **raspberries**

8 tablespoons **soy yoghurt**

maple syrup (optional)

1 Put the flax seeds in a small bowl with the water and leave to soak for 10 minutes.

2 Meanwhile, mix the almonds, quinoa flour and baking powder in a mixing bowl.

3 Add the soy milk, maple syrup and soaked flax seeds and mix together.

4 Heat the oil in a large frying pan and add the batter in small piles, approximately 2 tablespoons each. Allow them to brown lightly on one side and then turn to brown the other side.

5 Serve with the fruit, yoghurt and maple syrup.

RDA 100%

398kcal	14g	20g	5g	46g	18g	6g	0.2g
CALORIES	PROTEIN	FAT	SAT FAT	CARBS	SUGAR	FIBRE	SALT

£0.79 /PERSON · SERVES 10 · EASE ★★☆☆☆ · PREP 20 MINS · COOK 20 MINS · GF OPTION

CHOCOLATE GRANOLA

A chocolate lover's dream come true. Chocolate for breakfast!

GLUTEN-FREE OPTION: use GF puffed rice and oats.

WHERE ON EARTH: coconut chips can be found in the 'Nuts and Dried Fruit' section in supermarkets, or online. We buy ours in bulk from Healthy Supplies.

75g **100% cocoa solids chocolate**, see p215

4 tablespoons **maple syrup**

2 tablespoons **coconut oil**

2 tablespoons **water**

½ mug/90g **coconut sugar**

2 mugs/200g **oats**

2 mugs/100g **puffed, brown rice**

2 mugs/100g **coconut chips**

½ mug/75g **pecans**, roughly chopped

½ mug/100g **flaked almonds**

1 Preheat the oven to 170°C fan oven/190°C/ gas 5. Grease a large roasting tray.

2 Put the chocolate, maple syrup, coconut oil, water, and coconut sugar in a small saucepan and heat until the sugar has dissolved.

3 Put the oats, rice, coconut chips, pecans, and almonds in a large bowl.

4 Add the contents of the saucepan and mix together.

5 Spread out on the roasting tray and bake in the oven for 10 minutes.

6 Take out of the oven. Stir everything together, spread out again and return to the oven for a further 10 minutes.

7 Take out of the oven and leave to cool.

8 Once cooled, store in an airtight jar.

RDA 100%

375kcal	7g	26g	12g	37g	16g	6g	0.1g
GALORIES	PROTEIN	FAT	SAT FAT	CARBS	SUGAR	FIBRE	SALT

BANANA AND CHOCOLATE SUPER-BREAKFAST

This breakfast really is a super-breakfast, packed with lots of good fats, protein and fibre. Low on carbs and with good sugars coming from the bananas to give you energy.

2 **bananas**

¹/₃ mug/100ml **almond milk**

2 tablespoons **peanut butter**, see p211

2 tablespoons **cacao powder**

TOPPING

1 mug/80g **chocolate granola,** see p22

2 tablespoons **flaked almonds**

2 tablespoons **pumpkin seeds**

1 **banana**, sliced

1 Put the bananas, milk, peanut butter, and cacao powder in a blender and blitz until smooth. Pour into the bottom of the cereal bowls.

2 Put the granola, almonds, pumpkin seeds and the sliced banana on top. You can arrange them prettily, or not, but do enjoy.

RDA 100%

503kcal	20g	38g	10g	61g	46g	16g	0.2g
CALORIES	PROTEIN	FAT	SAT FAT	CARBS	SUGAR	FIBRE	SALT

PINK LADY GRANOLA

WHERE ON EARTH: coconut flakes can be found with the nuts and dried fruit, or online. We buy ours in bulk from Healthy Supplies.

GLUTEN-FREE OPTION: use GF oats.

½ mug/150ml **maple syrup**

2 tablespoons **coconut oil**

2 tablespoons **water**

2 mugs/200g **oats**

2 **Pink Lady apples**, cored and cut into small cubes

½ mug/100g **flaked almonds**

2 mugs/100g **coconut chips**

½ teaspoon **cinnamon**

¼ teaspoon **nutmeg**

12 **ready-to-eat dried apricots**, chopped

⅔ mug/100g **raisins**

1 Preheat the oven to 170°C fan oven/190°C/gas 5. Grease a large roasting tray.

2 Put the maple syrup, coconut oil and water in a small saucepan and heat until the coconut oil is melted.

3 Put the oats, apples, almonds, coconut chips, cinnamon and nutmeg in a large bowl.

4 Add the contents of the saucepan and mix together.

5 Spread out on the roasting tray and bake in the oven for 15 minutes.

6 Take out of the oven. Stir everything together, spread out again and return to the oven for a further 10 minutes.

7 Take out of the oven, add the apricots and raisins. Stir together, spread out and leave to cool.

8 Once cooled, store in an airtight jar.

RDA 100%

262kcal	5g	16g	9g	35g	18g	6.5g	0.2g
CALORIES	PROTEIN	FAT	SAT FAT	CARBS	SUGAR	FIBRE	SALT

QUINOA PORRIDGE

Tastes so good it could easily be a dessert after a meal!

WHERE ON EARTH: quinoa can be found in the 'Rice' section.

GLUTEN-FREE OPTION: use GF oats.

75g **quinoa**

½ mug/40g **oats**

1 mug/300ml **almond milk**

1 tablespoon **nutritional yeast**

1 teaspoon **vanilla bean paste**

20g **vegan margarine** (e.g. Tomor)

2 **Pink Lady apples**, cored and sliced

2 tablespoons **maple syrup**

1 teaspoon **cinnamon**

1 Put the quinoa in a small saucepan and cover with boiling water. Simmer for 10 minutes. Drain and return to the pan.

2 Add the oats, almond milk, nutritional yeast and vanilla bean paste and bring to the boil. Simmer for 2 minutes.

3 Meanwhile, heat the margarine in a medium frying pan, add the apples and fry for 3 minutes. Add the maple syrup and cinnamon and fry for a further 2 minutes.

4 Serve the fried apples with the porridge.

RDA 100%

| 434kcal | 10g | 19g | 5g | 50g | 28g | 7.5g | 1g |
| CALORIES | PROTEIN | FAT | SAT FAT | CARBS | SUGAR | FIBRE | SALT |

OVERNIGHT BIRCHER MUESLI

The 10 minute prep time could be seen as slightly misleading on this one, as you have to leave it overnight. Smugness guaranteed, though, if you prepare this the night before!

1 mug/100g **oats**

250g **vegan yoghurt**

⅓ mug/100ml **coconut milk**

juice and **zest of an orange**

200g **frozen blueberries**

2 tablespoons **toasted, chopped hazelnuts**

1 Mix the oats, yoghurt, coconut milk, orange zest, orange juice and frozen blueberries together.

2 Leave in the fridge overnight.

3 Sprinkle with chopped hazelnuts and serve.

RDA 100%

464kcal	13g	21g	7g	31g	14g	10.5g	0.4g
CALORIES	PROTEIN	FAT	SAT FAT	CARBS	SUGAR	FIBRE	SALT

BREAKFAST HASH

This recipe really benefits from our homemade tomato sauce. It's worth keeping a bottle of it in the fridge.

4 medium **potatoes**, cut into 3cm chunks

2 tablespoons **rapeseed oil**

2 **red onions**, chopped

250g **mushrooms**, sliced

2 x 400g tins **haricot beans**

coconut crisps, see p212 (Optional, but amazing)

tomato sauce, see p209 (optional)

1　Put the potatoes in a pan of boiling water, simmer for 8 minutes and drain.

2　Heat the oil in large frying pan, or wok. Add the potatoes and onions and fry until they begin to brown. Season well with salt and pepper.

3　Add the mushrooms and continue to fry.

4　Once the potatoes are browned, add the haricot beans and fry for 2–3 minutes. Add a little more oil if necessary.

5　Serve with the coconut crisps and tomato sauce.

RDA 100%

373kcal	10g	17g	6g	41g	13g	10g	1g
CALORIES	PROTEIN	FAT	SAT FAT	CARBS	SUGAR	FIBRE	SALT

SUPER SMOOTHIES

These are all 'one star' ratings for 'ease'. Just throw the ingredients into your blender and hit the 'go' button.

AVOCADO AND BANANA

1 ½ mugs/450ml **soy milk**

⅔ mug/200g **vegan yoghurt**

1 **avocado**

1 **banana**

100g **peanut butter**, see p211

3 tablespoons **maple syrup**

RDA 100%

TROPICAL

½ **mango**, peeled

1 mug/300ml **coconut drink**

juice of a **lime**

225g fresh **pineapple** pieces

25g **cashews**

add **apple juice** to get to your desired consistency

RDA 100%

MANGO AND RASPBERRY

½ **mango**, peeled

1 tablespoon freshly grated **ginger**

1 **kiwi fruit**, peeled

150g **raspberries**

1 mug/300ml **almond milk**

juice of a **lime**

1 tablespoon **hazelnut butter**, see p211

RDA 100%

SPIRULINA

1 **apple**, chopped

juice of a **lime**

1 teaspoon **spirulina**

½ mug/150ml **almond milk**

1 tablespoon **maple syrup**

1 tablespoon **cashew butter**, see p211

RDA 100%

SPINACH AND KALE

2 **bananas**

50g **kale**

30g **spinach**

1 mug/300ml **coconut drink**

RDA 100%

BLUEBERRY

150g **blueberries**

2 **apples**, peeled and cored

1 mug/300ml **apple juice**

2 tablespoons **hazelnut butter**, see p211

RDA 100%

LUNCH

£2.84 /PERSON · SERVES 4 · EASE ★★☆☆☆ · PREP 15 MINS · GF OPTION

PULLED JACKFRUIT BURRITOS

If you manage to eat this 'rolled up', without getting it everywhere, you deserve a medal.

WHERE ON EARTH: jackfruit can be found with the canned vegetables.

GLUTEN-FREE OPTION: use 'free-from' wraps and GF soy sauce.

2 tablespoons **rapeseed oil**

2 x 400g tins **jackfruit**, chopped

4 cloves **garlic**, chopped

3 tablespoons **soy sauce**

3 tablespoons **maple syrup**

2 tablespoons **tomato purée**

1 tablespoon **rapeseed oil**

1 **red pepper**, sliced

1 **onion**, sliced

400g tin **black beans**

4 **tortillas/wraps**

1 **Romaine lettuce**, thinly sliced

beetroot pickle, see p208

1 **fat red chilli**, sliced

1 Heat the oil in a large frying pan and add the chopped jackfruit and garlic. Fry for 2 minutes. Add the soy sauce, maple syrup and tomato purée and fry gently for about 5 minutes, the jackfruit will begin to fall apart. Set to one side until needed.

2 Heat the other tablespoon of oil in a frying pan and fry the peppers and onions until they begin to brown. Add the beans and heat through. Season well with salt and pepper.

3 Assemble the burrito and pile some of the beetroot pickle on top. Garnish with the sliced chilli.

RDA 100%

540kcal	16g	15g	2g	83g	17g	15g	3g
CALORIES	PROTEIN	FAT	SAT FAT	CARBS	SUGAR	FIBRE	SALT

CHERRY TOMATO TARTS & SWEET HASSELBACKS

From an RDA point of view, each person should only have one sweet potato. However, if you are anything like Ben, you will probably be tempted to stick another in the oven!

GLUTEN-FREE OPTION: use 'free-from' pastry.

4 medium **sweet potatoes**

2 tablespoons **rapeseed oil**

280g **vegan puff pastry**

soy cream to brush the pastry

6 tablespoons **soy cream**

2 tablespoons **cashew butter**, see p211

bunch **spring onions**, chopped

300g cherry **tomatoes**, halved

1 tablespoon **olive oil**

1 Preheat the oven to 200°c fan oven/220°C/gas 7.

2 Slice the potatoes, without going all the way through. Brush the tops of them with the oil and season with salt and pepper. Place on a greased, roasting tray and bake in the oven for 45 minutes.

3 Meanwhile, unroll the pastry and cut into 4 squares. Place on a large baking tray. Pinch the edges and then brush the pastry with a little soy cream.

4 Blind bake in the oven for 5 minutes.

5 Mix together the soy cream, cashew butter and the spring onions.

6 Take the tarts out of the oven and spread the onion mixture over them. Put the tomatoes on top, season with salt and pepper, and drizzle with oil.

7 Return to the oven and bake for 20 minutes. Serve with the potatoes.

RDA 100%

678kcal	8g	32g	9g	85g	19g	10g	1g
CALORIES	PROTEIN	FAT	SAT FAT	CARBS	SUGAR	FIBRE	SALT

PEPPER AND MUSHROOM BRUSCHETTA

If you are feeling really posh, you could cut the ciabatta into 8 and make it into a starter for 8 people.

GLUTEN-FREE OPTION: use GF ciabatta.

---

3 tablespoons **rapeseed oil**

2 **red onions**, sliced

2 **red peppers**, sliced

6 portobello **mushrooms**, sliced

2 tablespoons **balsamic vinegar**

½ mug/100g **pine nuts**

20 **black olives**, chopped

1 tablespoon freshly chopped **tarragon**

1 large **ciabatta**, cut into 4 and toasted

1   Heat the oil in a large frying pan. Add the onions and peppers and fry on a medium heat for 7–8 minutes. Things should begin to caramelise.

2   Add the mushrooms and fry for a further 3 minutes. Season well with salt and pepper.

3   Add the balsamic vinegar and the pine nuts. Heat for another 1 minute.

4   Stir in the olives and the fresh tarragon and serve with the toasted ciabatta.

RDA 100%

| 588kcal | 17g | 30g | 3g | 59g | 14g | 7g | 1g |
| CALORIES | PROTEIN | FAT | SAT FAT | CARBS | SUGAR | FIBRE | SALT |

£ 1.95 /PERSON · SERVES 4 · EASE ★★☆☆☆ · PREP 20 MINS · GF OPTION

FRIED TOFU WITH SPROUTED BEAN SALAD

Allowing time to marinate the tofu really pays off, as the flavours absorb beautifully, creating a lovely, sticky, sweet addition to the salad.

GLUTEN-FREE OPTION: use GF soy sauce.

2 x 280g packets **firm tofu**, sliced

4 tablespoons **soy sauce**

2 tablespoons **maple syrup**

1 tablespoon **rapeseed oil**

SPROUTED BEAN SALAD

330g jar Biona organic **bean sprouts**, rinsed and drained

½ **cucumber**, diced

1 **red onion**, thinly sliced

1 **Little Gem lettuce**, chopped

DRESSING

2 tablespoons **olive oil**

2 tablespoons **pomegranate molasses**

juice of a **lime**

salt and **pepper**

1 Put the tofu in a bowl and add the soy sauce, maple syrup and 1 tablespoon of oil. Season with plenty of pepper and leave to marinate for 10 minutes.

2 Place the bean salad ingredients in a large bowl and mix.

3 Mix the dressing ingredients together and add to the salad bowl.

4 Heat 2 tablespoons of oil in a large frying pan. Add the tofu, but not the marinade, and gently fry on each side until nicely browned. Add the marinade and continue to cook for 2 minutes.

5 Serve with the salad.

RDA 100%

| 402kcal | 21g | 27g | 3g | 18g | 13g | 4g | 4g |
| CALORIES | PROTEIN | FAT | SAT FAT | CARBS | SUGAR | FIBRE | SALT |

CARROT AND CASHEW NUT SOUP

It is worth keeping a store-cupboard stocked with some of the items (in this case the cashew butter) in the homemade section, at the back of this book, so they are at hand when you need them.

GLUTEN-FREE OPTION: use GF stock and GF bread.

2 tablespoons **rapeseed oil**

2 **onions**, sliced

1 clove **garlic**, chopped

5 **carrots**, peeled and sliced

4 tablespoons **cashew nut butter**, see p211

6 mugs/2 litres **water**

2 **veg stock cubes**

3 tablespoons freshly chopped **coriander**

crusty bread

1   Heat the oil in a large saucepan, add the onions and garlic, and fry until things just begin to brown.

2   Add the carrots and fry for 2 minutes. Season well with salt and pepper.

3   Add the cashew butter, water and stock. Bring to the boil and then turn down to simmer for 10 minutes.

4   Blend until smooth.

5   Stir in the coriander and serve with crusty bread.

RDA 100%

278kcal	6g	15g	3g	26g	16g	6g	0.3g
CALORIES	PROTEIN	FAT	SAT FAT	CARBS	SUGAR	FIBRE	SALT

ROAST VEG SOUP WITH CARAMELISED ONIONS

This soup is all about the accessories! Caramelised red onions give an extra shot of sweetness and the pumpkins seeds give crunch.

GLUTEN-FREE OPTION: use GF stock.

1 **butternut squash**, cut into chunks

6 **tomatoes**, halved

2 **parsnips**, cut into chunks

1 **red onion**, cut into wedges

2 **carrots**, cut into chunks

3 tablespoons **olive oil**

1 tablespoon **olive oil**

2 **red onions**, sliced

3 mugs/900ml **water**

2 **veg stock cubes**

2 tablespoons **sunflower seeds**

1 Preheat the oven to 180°C fan oven/200°C/gas 6.

2 Put the vegetables on a large roasting tray. Drizzle with the oil, season well and spread things out evenly.

3 Roast in the oven for 50 minutes, or until the vegetables are nicely browned.

4 10 minutes before the end of the cooking time, heat the oil in a small frying pan. Add the onions and season well. Fry gently until they are nicely browned.

5 Meanwhile, put 3 mugs of boiling water in a large saucepan and add the stock cubes.

6 Once the vegetables are roasted, add them to the saucepan and bring to the boil. Blitz the soup with a blender and serve with the onions and the sunflower seeds.

RDA 100%

| 356kcal | 6g | 16g | 2g | 43g | 29g | 10g | 1g |
| CALORIES | PROTEIN | FAT | SAT FAT | CARBS | SUGAR | FIBRE | SALT |

SWEETCORN CHOWDER

East meets West in this fusion soup, with the usual milk, or cream, being replaced by coconut milk. A shot of lime at the end gives a sharpness that really lifts this soup.

GLUTEN-FREE OPTION: use GF stock and GF bread.

---

2 tablespoons **olive oil**

1 **onion**, chopped

1 **red pepper**, chopped

1 **fat red chilli**, chopped

340g tin **sweetcorn**

2 mugs/600ml **water** + 2 **veg stock cubes**

400ml tin **coconut milk**

2 tablespoons freshly chopped **chives**

juice of a **lime**

crusty bread

1 Heat the oil in a large saucepan and add the onions, pepper and chilli. Fry for 2–3 minutes, or until the onions begin to soften.

2 Add the sweetcorn, water, stock cubes and coconut milk. Season well with salt and pepper. Bring to the boil and turn down to simmer for 5 minutes.

3 Mix in the chives and lime and serve with the bread.

RDA 100%

| 561kcal | 13g | 28g | 14g | 61g | 14g | 6g | 1g |
| CALORIES | PROTEIN | FAT | SAT FAT | CARBS | SUGAR | FIBRE | SALT |

READY-ROASTED RED PEPPER SOUP

A classic, simple soup. Quick and easy to make. We always try to use fresh tomatoes, rather than tinned tomatoes, as an easy way to avoid a processed product.

GLUTEN-FREE OPTION: use GF stock, soy sauce and bread.

---

1 tablespoon **olive oil**

1 **onion**, sliced

6 **tomatoes**, roughly chopped

3 cloves **garlic**, chopped

3 **ready-roasted red peppers**

1 mug/300ml **water**

1 **veg stock cube**

²/₃ mug/200ml **soy cream**

1 teaspoon **smoked paprika**

crusty bread to serve

1 Heat the oil in a large saucepan, add the onions and fry for 3–4 minutes until the onions begin to soften.

2 Add the tomatoes and fry for another 3–4 minutes.

3 Add the rest of the ingredients and bring to the boil. Season with salt and pepper and turn down to simmer for 5 minutes.

4 Blitz with a blender and serve with the bread.

RDA 100%

| 426kcal | 12g | 14g | 2g | 59g | 13g | 5g | 1g |
| CALORIES | PROTEIN | FAT | SAT FAT | CARBS | SUGAR | FIBRE | SALT |

£ 1.77 /PERSON | SERVES 4 | EASE ★☆☆☆☆ | PREP 15 MINS | COOK 20 MINS | GF OPTION

ACKEE ON TOAST

Ackee is actually a fruit, with origins in Jamaica, but is mainly used in savoury dishes and is great on toast.

WHERE ON EARTH: ackee can be found with the 'ready-made' sauces.

GLUTEN-FREE OPTION: use GF bread.

---

4 slices **bread**

1 tablespoon **olive oil**

bunch of **spring onions**, chopped

100g **cherry tomatoes**, halved

540g tin **ackee**, rinsed and drained

100g **spinach**

2 tablespoons freshly chopped **chives**

1 Toast the bread.

2 Heat the oil in a large frying pan. Add the onions and fry for 1 minute.

3 Add the tomatoes and fry for 3–4 minutes. Allow both to brown a little.

4 Add the ackee and fry for one minute, seasoning well with salt and pepper.

5 Add the spinach and chives and allow the spinach to wilt.

6 Serve on the toast.

RDA 100%

| 288kcal | 10g | 17g | 5g | 23g | 4g | 4g | 1g |
| CALORIES | PROTEIN | FAT | SAT FAT | CARBS | SUGAR | FIBRE | SALT |

NUTTY CARMARGUE RICE

The ECO friendly concept of 'cook once and eat twice' is one we like in the NOSH kitchen. This dish is a perfect example where you can cook one day and eat it hot, or cold, the next day.

1 ½ mugs/375g **Carmargue rice**

1 ½ teaspoons **cumin seeds**

3 tablespoons **sesame seeds**

3 tablespoons **pumpkin seeds**

2 tablespoons **olive oil**

400g **cherry tomatoes**

1 **fat red chilli**, chopped

3 **red onions**, cut into thin wedges

2 tablespoons **balsamic vinegar**

1 mug/150g **Brazil nuts**, roughly chopped

juice of a **lime**

1 Put the carmargue rice in a pan of boiling, salted water and simmer for 30 minutes.

2 Put the cumin, sesame and pumpkin seeds in a large frying pan, or wok, and dry-toast for 3–4 minutes on a gentle heat, or until the pumpkin seeds begin to pop.

3 Add the oil to the pan and the tomatoes, chilli and onions. Turn the heat up slightly and fry until the onions begins to brown.

4 Add the balsamic vinegar and fry for 1 minute.

5 Add the cooked rice to the pan, along with the Brazil nuts and lime juice. Season well with salt and pepper and stir gently to mix.

RDA 100%

642kcal	19g	37g	9g	54g	13g	8g	0.1g
CALORIES	PROTEIN	FAT	SAT FAT	CARBS	SUGAR	FIBRE	SALT

GREEN PANCAKES

There is a lovely, hidden element to this meal in the form of the tomato juice inside the cherry tomatoes that is ready to pop out when you dive in. Bibs are optional!

WHERE ON EARTH: almond milk is found with the 'long-life' juices.

GLUTEN-FREE OPTION: use GF flour.

---

1 tablespoon **ground flax seeds**

3 tablespoons **water**

PANCAKES

1 mug/300ml **almond milk**

100g **spinach**

2 tablespoons freshly chopped **basil**

200g **self-raising flour**

juice of a **lemon**

1 tablespoon **coconut oil** to fry the pancakes

½ mug/100g **cashews**

400g **cherry tomatoes**

250g **chestnut mushrooms**

2 tablespoons **coconut oil** to fry the cashews and tomatoes, etc.

1 Mix the flax seeds and water in a small bowl. Leave to stand for 10 minutes.

2 Put the pancake ingredients in a blender, or food processor. Blitz until smooth. Add the flax seeds, season well with salt and pepper, and pulse a few times.

3 Heat the coconut oil in a frying pan. Put a quarter of the mixture in the pan and swirl around to spread slightly. Cook gently until the bottom of the pancake is browned and then flip over. Repeat until all four pancakes are cooked.

4 Meanwhile, in another frying pan, heat the coconut oil and add the cashews, tomatoes and mushrooms. Fry until things begin to brown. Season well with salt and pepper.

5 Serve with the pancakes.

RDA 100%

540kcal	13g	30g	14g	51g	6g	4g	1g
CALORIES	PROTEIN	FAT	SAT FAT	CARBS	SUGAR	FIBRE	SALT

MISO GLAZED AUBERGINE

This is a great meal to make for friends. It's a bit 'posh' looking, but really easy to make, as, basically, you just pop it in the oven, make the salad and serve.

WHERE ON EARTH: preserved lemons are in the 'Canned Fruit' section.

GLUTEN-FREE OPTION: use GF soy sauce.

---

2 large **aubergines**

GLAZE
2 tablespoons **miso paste**
1 tablespoon **maple syrup**
1 tablespoon **soy sauce**
1 tablespoon **toasted sesame oil**
1 tablespoon freshly grated **ginger**
1 clove **garlic**, chopped

2 tablespoons **olive oil**
½ mug/100g **cashews**
2 teaspoons **cumin seeds**
4 **carrots**, grated
1 **preserved lemon**, finely chopped
½ mug/70g **raisins**

Romaine lettuce
juice of a **lemon**
1 tablespoon **maple syrup**
4 **spring onions**, thinly sliced
1 tablespoon **sesame seeds**

1 Preheat the oven to 180°C fan oven/200°C/ gas 6.

2 Grease a roasting tray. Cut the aubergines in half lengthways and place on the roasting tray. Mix together the glaze and season with salt and pepper. Spread evenly over the cut surfaces of the aubergines and roast in the oven for 35 minutes.

3 Meanwhile, make the salad. Heat the oil in a medium frying pan, add the cashews and cumin seeds and fry until the nuts are lightly browned. Tip into a large mixing bowl, including all the oil. Add the carrots, lemon and raisins and combine.

4 Thinly slice the lettuce and mix with the lemon juice and maple syrup. Divide between the plates.

5 Sprinkle the spring onions and sesame seeds on top of the aubergines and serve with the lettuce and the carrot salad.

RDA 100%

| 422kcal | 11g | 27g | 5g | 39g | 20g | 9g | 2g |
| CALORIES | PROTEIN | FAT | SAT FAT | CARBS | SUGAR | FIBRE | SALT |

BLACK BEAN AND AVOCADO TOASTIE

A twist on the classic avocado on toast, this little lunch packs an energy punch, with most of it coming from the avocados.

GLUTEN-FREE OPTION: use GF bread.

2 slices **bread/ciabatta**

2 **avocados**

2 tablespoons **rapeseed oil**

1 **red onion**, sliced

100g **cherry tomatoes**, halved

½ x 400g tin **black beans**, rinsed and drained

juice of a **lemon**

1 tablespoon freshly chopped **coriander** to serve

1 Toast the bread/ciabatta.

2 Peel and squash the avocados with a fork. Spread on the toast.

3 Heat the oil in a medium frying pan and fry the onions and tomatoes for 2 minutes.

4 Add the beans and fry for 1 minute.

5 Add the lemon juice and stir together. Season with salt and pepper.

6 Serve the onion mix on top of the toast, with the coriander sprinkled over.

RDA 100%

543kcal	10g	36g	6g	41g	10g	14g	0.5g
CALORIES	PROTEIN	FAT	SAT FAT	CARBS	SUGAR	FIBRE	SALT

STUFFED MUSHROOMS WITH APPLE SLAW

We love ginger, in fact 75% of us in the NOSH family are ginger - so don't neglect the ginger, OK!

WHERE ON EARTH: pumpkin seeds are with the nuts and dried fruit.

GLUTEN-FREE OPTION: use GF soy sauce and GF bread.

---

8 **portobello mushrooms**

2 tablespoons **olive oil**

1 **onion**, chopped

2 cloves **garlic**, chopped

2 tablespoons freshly grated **ginger**

1 **red pepper**, chopped

1 tablespoon **soy sauce**

2 slices **bread**, made into breadcrumbs

200g packet **vegan cream cheese**

SLAW

3 tablespoons **vegan mayo**

juice of a **lemon**

1 **Romaine heart lettuce**, thinly sliced

2 **red apples**, thinly sliced

bunch **spring onions**, thinly sliced

50g **peanuts**

2 tablespoons **pumpkin seeds**

1 Preheat the grill.

2 Take the stalks out of the mushrooms and chop the stalks finely. Place the mushrooms on a roasting tray, drizzle with olive oil and season with salt and pepper.

3 Heat the oil in a frying pan and add the onions, garlic, ginger, chopped mushroom stalks and peppers. Fry for 3 minutes and take off the heat.

4 Mix in the soy sauce, breadcrumbs and cream cheese.

5 Divide the mixture between the mushrooms and put the mushrooms under the grill for about 10 minutes. The tops will begin to brown lightly.

6 Meanwhile, mix the mayo and lemon juice together and then add the rest of the slaw ingredients and mix.

7 Serve with the mushrooms.

RDA 100%

542kcal	15g	36g	14g	38g	19g	8g	2g
CALORIES	PROTEIN	FAT	SAT FAT	CARBS	SUGAR	FIBRE	SALT

PESTO GNOCCHI WITH FRIED ASPARAGUS

There is one person in particular (Ron) in the NOSH family who constantly says 'gnocchi' completely wrong. We know there are 75 ways to pronounce it, but not one of them is the way he says it; it seems to be a blend of French, Chinese and Geordie, which obviously doesn't sound Italian in the slightest.

Super-easy recipe for when you fancy something 'like pasta', but want a change.

WHERE ON EARTH: gnocchi is with the fresh pasta.

GLUTEN-FREE OPTION: use GF gnocchi.

---

2 x 400g packets **vegan gnocchi**

2 tablespoons **olive oil**

400g **asparagus**, with thick ends snapped off

PESTO

50g fresh **basil**

½ mug/100g **cashews**

4 tablespoons **olive oil**

juice of 2 **lemons**

2 tablespoons **maple syrup**

½ mug/150ml **water** from cooking the gnocchi

1 Put the gnocchi in a pan of boiling, salted water and simmer until the gnocchi start to float to the top. Drain (keep ½ a mug of the liquid for later) and return to the pan.

2 Heat the oil in a large frying pan, add the asparagus and fry on a medium heat for 3–4 minutes. Keep turning them to make sure they cook evenly and are lightly browned. Season well with salt and pepper.

3 Put the pesto ingredients in a blender and blitz. Add to the gnocchi pan, together with the ½ mug of cooking liquid, and mix.

4 Heat gently for 1 minute. Serve with the asparagus.

RDA 100%

| 690kcal | 11g | 34g | 5g | 84g | 7g | 3g | 3g |
| CALORIES | PROTEIN | FAT | SAT FAT | CARBS | SUGAR | FIBRE | SALT |

KIBBEH WITH AVOCADO DIP

Kibbeh is a national dish of Lebanon. The blue corn chips used here might not be available in all supermarkets, but they are worth trying to find, if you can. They not only look fun, but are actually a little more healthy than their pale counterparts.

BUTTERNUT KIBBEH

1 tablespoon **flax seeds**

3 tablespoons **water**

1/2 **butternut squash**, peeled and cut in 3cm chunks

250g packet **cooked quinoa**

1 teaspoon **ground coriander**

1 teaspoon **cumin**

1 teaspoon **sumac**

1 teaspoon **paprika**

1/2 **teaspoon nutmeg**

4 tablespoons **ground almonds**

2 tablespoons freshly chopped **parsley**

1 **red onion**, chopped

juice of a **lemon**

AVOCADO DIP

2 **avocados**

2 tablespoons **tahini**

juice of a **lemon**

1 teaspoon **maple syrup**

1 teaspoon **cumin seeds**

2 tablespoons freshly chopped **basil**

1/2 mug/85g **pine nuts**, to sprinkle on top

blue corn chips

celery

mixed carrots

1 Preheat the oven to 180°C fan oven/200°C/gas 6. Grease a large roasting tray.

2 Mix together the flax seeds and the water. Leave to stand for 10 minutes.

3 Meanwhile, put the squash in a pan of boiling water and simmer for 5 minutes. Drain and mash. Season with salt and pepper.

4 Add the rest of the kibbeh ingredients, including the flax seeds, and mix together.

5 Form into 16 balls and place on the roasting tray. Bake in the oven for 25 minutes.

6 Put the avocado dip ingredients in a food processor, or blender, and blitz until smooth. Sprinkle over with the pine nuts.

7 Serve together with the dip and the veg, chopped into sticks.

RDA 100%

| 928kcal | 25g | 54g | 7g | 74g | 25g | 18g | 1g |
| CALORIES | PROTEIN | FAT | SAT FAT | CARBS | SUGAR | FIBRE | SALT |

ROASTED BEETROOT SALAD

If you have time for the veg to roast in the oven, this recipe is well worth the wait.

WHERE ON EARTH: wasabi paste is with the spices, or mustards and condiments.

500g **raw beetroot**, peeled and cut into wedges

4 **parsnips**, peeled and cut into sticks

4 medium **carrots**, peeled and cut into sticks

2 **red onions**, peeled and cut into wedges

3 tablespoons **olive oil**

1 tablespoon **maple syrup**

50g **pine nuts**

bag of **rocket salad**

COCONUT SAUCE

⅓ mug/100ml **coconut cream**

1 teaspoon **wasabi paste**

juice of a **lemon**

1 Preheat the oven to 180°C fan oven/200°C/gas 6.

2 Put the beets, parsnips, carrots and onions on a large roasting tray. Drizzle over the oil, season well with salt and pepper, and mix everything together. Spread out evenly and roast in the oven for 55 minutes. Drizzle over with the maple syrup.

3 Serve with a sprinkle of pine nuts and a drizzle of the combined, coconut sauce ingredients.

70

RDA 100%

| 548kcal | 11g | 35g | 17g | 42g | 31g | 14g | 1g |
| CALORIES | PROTEIN | FAT | SAT FAT | CARBS | SUGAR | FIBRE | SALT |

DINNER

£1.56 /PERSON — SERVES 14 — EASE ★★☆☆☆ — PREP 15 MINS — GF OPTION

VEGETABLE PILAU WITH A MINT RAITA

The raisins and cashews in this vegetable pilau are a nice combination of sweet and savoury, together with the contrast in being chewy and crunchy.

GLUTEN-FREE OPTION: use GF stock.

2 tablespoons **olive oil**

2 **onions**, sliced

1 **red pepper**, diced

2 cloves **garlic**, chopped

2 tablespoons freshly grated **ginger**

1 mug/250g **basmati rice**

1 teaspoon **cumin**

1 teaspoon **coriander**

2 mugs/600ml **water** + 2 **veg stock cubes**

1 **fat red chilli**, chopped

2 mugs/320g **frozen edamame beans**, defrosted

⅓ mug/60g **raisins**

½ mug/100g **cashews**

freshly chopped **coriander**, to serve

RAITA

⅓ mug/200ml **vegan yoghurt**

½ **cucumber**, grated

2 tablespoons freshly chopped **mint**

1 Heat the oil in a large frying pan, or wok. Add the onion, red pepper, garlic and ginger and fry until the onions begin to brown. Add the rice and fry for 1 minute. Season well with salt and pepper.

2 Add the cumin, coriander, water and stock cubes and bring to the boil. Turn down to simmer with a lid on the pan for 8 minutes.

3 Meanwhile, mix together the raita ingredients.

4 Add the chilli, edamame beans, raisins and cashews and leave to simmer for 2 minutes, with the lid on the pan.

5 Take off the heat and add the coriander. Serve with the raita.

RDA 100%

498kcal	23g	25g	4g	61g	12g	10g	1g
CALORIES	PROTEIN	FAT	SAT FAT	CARBS	SUGAR	FIBRE	SALT

BELUGA LENTILS IN A SWEET PEANUT SAUCE

If you haven't already checked out our home-made 'nut butters' on p211 take a look. It means you know exactly what you are eating, rather than chancing the shop-bought variety.

WHERE ON EARTH: beluga lentils are with the tinned beans.

GLUTEN-FREE OPTION: use GF soy sauce.

---

1 mug/250g **basmati rice**

200g **sugar snaps**

1 mug/180g **frozen peas**, defrosted

2 tablespoons **sesame oil**

1 **onion**, sliced

2 cloves **garlic**, chopped

2 **courgettes**, sliced

1 **fat red chilli**, chopped

2 tablespoons freshly grated **ginger**

250g **ready-to-eat beluga lentils**

100g **spinach**

SAUCE

150g **peanut butter**, see p211

2 tablespoons **soy sauce**

juice of a **lime**

1 tablespoon **maple syrup**

½ mug/150ml **water**

1 Put the rice in a pan with 2 mugs of boiling water. Bring to the boil and then turn down to simmer, with a lid on the pan, for 9 minutes.

2 Add the sugar snaps and peas to the rice, put the lid back onto the pan, and simmer for 1 minute. Set aside until needed.

3 Meanwhile, heat the oil in a wok, or large frying pan. Add the onions, garlic and courgettes and fry until they begin to brown. Add the chilli and ginger and fry for 1 minute.

4 Add the lentils and spinach and fry for 1 minute.

5 Mix together the sauce ingredients and add to the wok. Bring to the boil and simmer for 2 minutes.

6 Stir the sugar snaps and peas into the rice and serve with the peanut lentils.

RDA 100%

521kcal	26g	27g	5g	42g	11g	12g	1g
CALORIES	PROTEIN	FAT	SAT FAT	CARBS	SUGAR	FIBRE	SALT

BLACK-EYED BEAN BURGERS

So this recipe should all be about the burger, right? As good as the burger is, don't ignore this salad. It is so good you should use it, with something else, another time.

GLUTEN-FREE OPTION: use GF soy sauce and GF bread.

BURGER

1 tablespoon **flax seeds**

3 tablespoons **water**

75g **peanuts**

1 slice **bread**

1 tablespoon freshly grated **ginger**

400g tin **black-eyed beans**

2 tablespoons freshly chopped **coriander**

1 tablespoon **soy sauce**

1 **fat red chilli**, chopped

1 **sweet potato**, peeled and grated

SALAD

50g blanched **almonds**, roughly chopped

2 **Granny Smith apples**, sliced

10 **medjool dates**, sliced

1 **Romaine lettuce**, sliced

DRESSING

juice of a **lemon**

1 tablespoon **extra virgin olive oil**

1 tablespoon **maple syrup**

1 Mix together the flax seeds and water and leave for 10 minutes.

2 Put the burger ingredients in a food processor, season well with salt and pepper and blitz. Add the flax seeds and pulse a couple of times.

3 Combine the salad ingredients.

4 Mix together the dressing ingredients and add to the salad.

5 Form the burger mixture into 8 burgers. Heat the oil in a large frying pan and fry the burgers on a medium heat until both sides are nicely browned.

6 Serve with the salad.

RDA 100%

798kcal	23g	45g	6g	73g	45g	13g	1g
CALORIES	PROTEIN	FAT	SAT FAT	CARBS	SUGAR	FIBRE	SALT

£ 1.82 /PERSON   SERVES 4   EASE ★★★☆☆   PREP 10 MINS   COOK 20 MINS   GF OPTION

APRICOT AND CHESTNUT MUSHROOM BURGERS

WHERE ON EARTH: milled flax seeds are in the 'Baking' section.

GLUTEN-FREE OPTION: use GF bread.

BURGERS

1 tablespoon **milled flax seeds** + 3 tablespoons **water**

250g **chestnut mushrooms**

1 **onion**

2 slices **bread**

1 teaspoon **cumin**

1 teaspoon **coriander**

1 teaspoon **cinnamon**

10 **ready-to-eat apricots**

½ mug/100g **peanuts**

2 tablespoons **olive oil**

SALAD

200g **kale**

2 tablespoons **tahini**

juice of a **lime**

2 tablespoons **water**

2 **Granny Smiths**, cut into matchsticks

⅔ mug/100g **pine nuts**

hot chilli sauce, see p217

1   Put the flax seeds and water in a small bowl and leave for 10 minutes.

2   Put the burger ingredients in a food processor and blitz until you have something resembling breadcrumbs, but not too fine. Add the flax seed mix, season well with salt and pepper and pulse a couple of times. Form into 4 burgers.

3   Heat the oil in a frying pan and fry the burgers until they are browned on each side.

4   Put the kale in a large frying pan and add half a mug of water. Bring to the boil and then turn down to simmer, with a lid on the pan, for 5 minutes. Take off the heat.

5   Add the rest of the salad ingredients to the pan and combine.

6   Serve with the burgers and some chilli sauce.

RDA 100%

672kcal CALORIES	25g PROTEIN	40g FAT	5g SAT FAT	47g CARBS	31g SUGAR	14g FIBRE	1g SALT

FALAFEL WITH HOT SAMBAL

Sambal may seem like a 'faff' to make, but it's the star of the show here and you can keep it in the fridge for about a month. In fact, I think Joy may still be using some she made 3 months ago!

GLUTEN-FREE OPTION: use GF flour.

RICE SALAD

¾ mug/190g **mixed rice**

½ mug/75g **pistachios**, chopped

125g **pomegranate seeds**

bunch **spring onions**, chopped

2 tablespoons freshly chopped **coriander**

juice of a **lemon**

2 tablespoons **olive oil**

1 tablespoon **maple syrup**

FALAFEL

1 medium **potato**, cut into chunks

2 ½ mugs/400g **frozen edamame beans**, defrosted

½ **onion**

1 clove **garlic**

1 tablespoon **ground coriander**

2 teaspoons **cumin**

1 teaspoon **paprika**

juice of ½ **lemon**

2 tablespoons **flour**

2 tablespoons freshly chopped **coriander**

oil to fry

sambal, see p210

1 Put the rice in a small pan of boiling, salted water. Simmer for 30 minutes with a lid on. Drain and add the rest of the salad ingredients. Season well.

2 Put the potato in a small pan of boiling, salted water. Simmer for 6 minutes. Drain and return to the pan.

3 Put the beans, onion and garlic in a food processor and blitz until you have something resembling breadcrumbs. Add the potato and pulse a few times. Add the rest of the falafel ingredients, season well and pulse a few times.

4 Form into 24 small balls. Flatten each one down slightly.

5 Heat the oil in a large frying pan and add the falafel. Fry on each side for 3–4 minutes until nicely browned.

6 Serve with the rice salad and sambal.

RDA 100%

592kcal	22g	25g	4g	65g	13g	17g	2g
CALORIES	PROTEIN	FAT	SAT FAT	CARBS	SUGAR	FIBRE	SALT

WILD RICE SALAD AND SWEET PEANUT DRESSING

Pomegranate molasses has a fantastic, sweet, piquant flavour, which is quite unusual.

WHERE ON EARTH: pomegranate molasses can be found in the 'Speciality Ingredients' section. If you can't find it where you shop you might need to get it online.

GLUTEN-FREE OPTION: use GF soy sauce.

RICE SALAD

1 mug/250g **wild rice**

½ medium **red cabbage**, thinly sliced

4 **carrots**, grated

330g jar **Biona bean sprouts**, drained and rinsed

½ **pineapple**, cut into chunks

bunch **spring onions**, chopped

3 tablespoons freshly chopped **coriander**

½ mug/100g **peanuts**

2 tablespoons **sesame seeds**

DRESSING

4 tablespoons **peanut butter**, see p211

¼ mug/75ml **almond milk**

¼ mug/75ml **water**

3 tablespoons **soy sauce**

1 tablespoon **pomegranate molasses**

1 tablespoon **maple syrup**

1 teaspoon **harissa paste**

juice of a **lemon**

1 Put the rice in a pan of boiling, salted water and simmer for 35–40 minutes.

2 Put the rest of the salad ingredients in a large bowl, along with the cooked rice, and mix together. Season well with salt and pepper.

3 Mix together the dressing ingredients in a saucepan. Gently heat and bring to the boil. Take off the heat.

4 Serve the salad with the sauce drizzled over generously.

RDA 100%

725kcal	28g	33g	6g	73g	28g	15g	2g
CALORIES	PROTEIN	FAT	SAT FAT	CARBS	SUGAR	FIBRE	SALT

MUSHROOM ROTOLO

OK, for those foodies out there, this is strictly speaking not a rotolo - they are normally round and made with pasta - but this is an easier alternative which tastes great!

WHERE ON EARTH: dried porcini mushrooms are in the 'Speciality Ingredients' section.

GLUTEN-FREE OPTION: use GF stock and soy sauce.

40g **dried porcini mushrooms**

2 tablespoons **rapeseed oil**

1 **red onion**, chopped

500g **chestnut mushrooms**, chopped

2 tablespoons **soy sauce**

4 **potatoes**, thinly sliced

¼ mug/75ml **boiling water** +
1 **veg stock cube**

2 tablespoons **rapeseed oil**

2 **carrots**, cut into thin strips using a peeler

200g **kale**

1   Put the porcini mushrooms in a bowl, cover with boiling water and soak for 20 minutes. Drain and chop.

2   Preheat the oven to 180°C fan oven/200°C/gas 6. Grease a casserole dish.

3   Heat the oil in a frying pan, add the onions and fry until they begin to soften. Add all the mushrooms and fry for 3 minutes. Season well, add the soy sauce and stir.

4   Arrange half the sliced potatoes in the bottom of the casserole dish. Put the mushroom mixture on top and then arrange the rest of the potatoes on top. Season.

5   Put the stock cube in the boiling water and then pour over the dish. Drizzle the top with more rapeseed oil.

6   Cover with foil and bake in the oven for 25 minutes.

7   Remove the foil and bake for a further 40 minutes.

8   10 minutes before the end of the cooking time, heat the oil in a frying pan. Add the carrots and allow to cook until they are lightly browned. Drain on some kitchen towel. You may need to cook them in batches.

9   Put the kale in a large frying pan, or wok, add ¼ mug of water and simmer for 3 minutes. Serve.

RDA 100%

372kcal	11g	16g	1g	41g	9g	10g	2g
CALORIES	PROTEIN	FAT	SAT FAT	CARBS	SUGAR	FIBRE	SALT

SWEET CHILLI TOFU NOODLES

Don't be afraid of browning your tofu really well, the more caramelised it is, the more intense the flavour.

GLUTEN-FREE OPTION: use GF soy sauce.

280g packet **firm tofu**

2 tablespoons **soy sauce**

2 tablespoons **maple syrup**

200g **rice noodles**

2 **carrots**, cut into matchsticks

2 tablespoons **toasted sesame oil**

bunch **spring onions**, chopped

½ mug/100g unsalted **peanuts**

200g **sugar snaps**, halved lengthways

6 tablespoons **sweet chilli sauce**, see p206

juice of a **lime**

2 tablespoons **soy sauce**

2 tablespoons freshly chopped **mint**

2 tablespoons freshly chopped **coriander**

1 Cut the tofu into 2cm cubes and place in a bowl with the soy sauce and maple syrup. Leave to stand for 10 minutes.

2 Put the noodles and carrots in a large bowl and pour over enough boiling water to cover. Leave to stand for 10 minutes.

3 Meanwhile, heat the sesame oil in a wok. Drain the tofu and add to the pan. Fry until it is browned on as many sides as possible. Remove from the pan and set to one side.

4 Add the onions, peanuts and sugar snaps to the pan and fry for 1 minute, or until the peanuts begin to brown.

5 Add the rest of the ingredients and mix together. Return the tofu to the pan and heat together for 1 minute.

6 Serve on top of the drained noodles and carrots.

RDA 100%

603kcal	24g	24g	4g	68g	24g	6g	4g
CALORIES	PROTEIN	FAT	SAT FAT	CARBS	SUGAR	FIBRE	SALT

LENTIL BOLOGNESE WITH SALSA VERDE

We have used quinoa spaghetti because it is a great source of protein. If you can't find any in your local supermarket you can use normal pasta and just cook according to the packet instructions.

GLUTEN-FREE OPTION: make sure you use GF spaghetti, stock and soy sauce.

300g **quinoa spaghetti**

2 tablespoons **olive oil**

1 **onion**, peeled and chopped

2 cloves **garlic**, chopped

400g **chestnut mushrooms**, chopped

6 **tomatoes**, chopped

400g tin **lentils**

1 **veg stock cube**

1 tablespoon **soy sauce**

1 tablespoon **balsamic vinegar**

1/3 mug/100ml **water**

2 tablespoons **tomato purée**

2 tablespoons freshly chopped **basil**

2 tablespoons **salsa verde**, see p214 (optional)

1 Put the spaghetti in a large pan of boiling, salted water and simmer gently for 12 minutes. Drain and rinse in hot water. This will stop it sticking together.

2 Meanwhile, heat the oil in a large frying pan, or wok. Add the onion and garlic and fry until the onions begin to brown a little.

3 Add the mushrooms and fry for 2 minutes.

4 Add the tomatoes and lentils and fry for 1 minute.

5 Add the stock cube, soy sauce, balsamic vinegar, water and tomato purée and simmer for 2 minutes. Season.

6 Add the basil and stir in.

7 Serve with the spaghetti and salsa verde.

RDA 100%

476kcal	16g	9g	1g	76g	10g	8g	1g
CALORIES	PROTEIN	FAT	SAT FAT	CARBS	SUGAR	FIBRE	SALT

MAPLE LEMON TOFU

This is a great way to cook. The broccolli will cook really quickly by blitzing it up and placing it on top of the rice as the rice cooks.

GLUTEN-FREE OPTION: use GF soy sauce.

1 mug/250g **basmati rice**

1 head **broccoli**

2 tablespoons **cornflour**

2 tablespoons **Chinese five spice**

365g pack **firm tofu**, chopped into chunks

2 tablespoons **toasted sesame oil**

1 **onion**, chopped

1 clove **garlic**, chopped

SAUCE

⅓ mug/100ml **maple syrup**

juice of a **lemon**

1 tablespoon **toasted sesame oil**

2 tablespoons **soy sauce**

1 mug/300ml **water** + 2 tablespoons **cornflour**

1 Put the rice in 2 mugs of boiling water. Simmer gently, with a lid on the pan, for 10 minutes.

2 Cut the florets from the broccoli and place in a food processor. Blitz until you have something resembling breadcrumbs.

3 Once the rice has been cooking for 8 minutes, add the broccoli to the top of the rice. Don't stir. Replace the lid and allow the rice to finish cooking. Once cooked, stir the broccoli through the rice.

4 Meanwhile, mix the cornflour and Chinese 5 spice together. Toss the tofu in the spice mix.

5 Heat the oil in a frying pan and fry the tofu until it is browned on as many sides as possible. Remove from the pan.

6 Add the onions and garlic to the pan and fry for 2 minutes. Season well with salt and pepper.

7 Mix together the sauce ingredients and add to the pan. Bring to the boil.

8 Put the tofu and the sauce over the top.

RDA 100%

378kcal	18g	18g	3g	39g	19g	4g	2g
CALORIES	PROTEIN	FAT	SAT FAT	CARBS	SUGAR	FIBRE	SALT

SWEDE RISOTTO WITH COCONUT CRISPS

Adding the coconut crisps to this recipe makes all the difference. We've had a jar of these in our storecupboard for 3 months and they are great for adding to various dishes to give that bit of crunch.

GLUTEN-FREE OPTION: use GF stock.

---

2 tablespoons **olive oil**

2 **onions**, chopped

1 **swede**, peeled and chopped

1 mug/250g **basmati rice**

400ml tin **coconut milk** + ²/₃ mug/200ml **water**

1 **veg stock cube**

4 tablespoons **Korma curry paste**

200g **spinach**, roughly chopped

2 tablespoons freshly chopped **coriander**

coconut crisps, see p212

1 Heat the oil in a wok. Add the onion and swede and fry for 3 minutes.

2 Add the rice and fry for 1 minute

3 Add the coconut milk, water, stock cube and curry paste. Bring to the boil. Turn down to simmer, with a lid on the pan, for 10 minutes.

4 Stir in the spinach and coriander. Take off the heat; the spinach will wilt in the heat from the pan.

5 Serve with the coconut crisps.

RDA 100%

| 389kcal | 7g | 27g | 14g | 33g | 17g | 7g | 1g |
| CALORIES | PROTEIN | FAT | SAT FAT | CARBS | SUGAR | FIBRE | SALT |

BELUGA LENTIL AND MUSHROOM BALLS

Ben would like us to point out that these are not in fact totally burnt! The beluga lentils give a very striking 'dark look' to this meal, which is fun.

GLUTEN-FREE OPTION: use GF soy sauce and GF spaghetti.

1 **carrot**, peeled and sliced

1 **onion**

3 slices of **bread**

150g **chestnut mushrooms**, finely chopped

1 tablespoon freshly chopped **basil**

250g **ready-to-eat-beluga lentils**, rinsed and drained

1 tablespoon **soy sauce**

2 tablespoons **tomato purée**

250g **quinoa spaghetti**

TOMATO SAUCE

6 **tomatoes**

2 tablespoons **tomato purée**

1 **red onion**

2 tablespoons freshly chopped **basil**

1 tablespoon **balsamic vinegar**

1 tablespoon **maple syrup**

1 tablespoon **cornflour**

1 Preheat the oven to 180°C fan oven/200°C/ gas 6. Grease and line a roasting tray.

2 Put the carrots, onion and bread in a food processor and blitz till you have something resembling breadcrumbs. Add the mushrooms and basil and pulse a few times. Add the lentils, soy sauce and tomato purée and pulse a couple of times .

3 Form into 25–30 small balls. Place on the roasting tray and bake in the oven for 25 minutes.

4 10 minutes before the end of the cooking time for the lentil balls, put the spaghetti on to cook.

5 Meanwhile, put the sauce ingredients in a food processor, or blender, and blitz until smooth. Season well. Put in a small saucepan, bring to the boil and simmer for 10 minutes.

RDA 100%

527kcal	22g	4g	1g	93g	18g	12g	1g
CALORIES	PROTEIN	FAT	SAT FAT	CARBS	SUGAR	FIBRE	SALT

£ 3.15 /PERSON | SERVES 4 | EASE ★★★☆☆ | PREP 10 MINS | COOK 50 MINS | GF OPTION

GOLDEN BEETROOT AND ORANGE SALAD

Golden beetroot tends to be a little sweeter than the red variety and a little more mellow. It works really well in salads when roasted.

4 medium **potatoes**, unpeeled and cut into 2cm chunks

2 tablespoons **olive oil**

1 teaspoon **smoked paprika**

1 teaspoon **cumin**

400g **golden beets**, peeled and cut into wedges

bunch **red beetroot**, peeled and cut into wedges

1 red **onion**, cut into wedges

125g **whole hazelnuts**

2 tablespoons **olive oil**

400g tin **cannellini beans**, rinsed and drained

340g tin **sweetcorn**, drained

1 tablespoon **olive oil**

zest and juice of a **lemon**

3 tablespoons freshly chopped **coriander**

2 **oranges**, peeled and sliced

1 Preheat the oven to 180°C fan oven/200°C/gas 6.

2 Put the potatoes on a roasting tray and drizzle over the oil. Add the paprika and cumin. Season with salt and pepper and mix together. Spread out evenly on the tray and roast in the oven for 50 minutes.

3 Put the golden beets, beetroot, onion and hazelnuts on another large roasting tray. Season well with salt and pepper, drizzle over the oil and mix everything together. Spread out and roast in the oven for 35 minutes.

4 After 35 minutes, take out of the oven and stir in the beans and sweetcorn. Return to the oven for another 10 minutes.

5 Once the beet mixture is cooked, drizzle over with the oil, lemon juice and zest. Add the coriander and oranges and gently stir. Serve with the potatoes.

RDA 100%

715kcal	18g	29g	4g	64g	30g	15g	0.75g
CALORIES	PROTEIN	FAT	SAT FAT	CARBS	SUGAR	FIBRE	SALT

PEANUT NOODLES

Really quick to make. The sugar snaps and peanuts make for a fresh, crunchy dish.

GLUTEN-FREE OPTION: use GF stock and soy sauce.

200g **rice noodles**

1 tablespoon **olive oil**
½ mug/100g **peanuts**
bunch **spring onions**, chopped
2 cloves **garlic**, chopped
1 **fat red chilli**, chopped
2 tablespoons freshly grated **ginger**
1 red **pepper**, diced
200g **sugar snaps**, halved

SAUCE

3 tablespoons **peanut butter**, see p211
3 tablespoons **soy sauce**
1 tablespoon **maple syrup**
1 teaspoon **cornflour**
1 mug/300ml **water**
1 **veg stock cube**

fresh coriander to serve

1 Cover the rice noodles in a large bowl of boiling water and leave to stand for 10 minutes. Drain and return to the bowl.

2 Meanwhile, heat the oil in a wok. Add the peanuts, spring onions, garlic, chilli, ginger and pepper and fry for 3 minutes.

3 Add the sugar snaps and fry for 1 minute. Season well with salt and pepper.

4 Mix the sauce ingredients together until smooth and add to the wok. Bring to the boil.

5 Serve on top of the noodles and sprinkle over the coriander. (You can see we forgot to add the coriander here, but you should definitely still do it!!)

RDA 100%

570kcal	21g	28g	4g	62g	9g	7g	2g
CALORIES	PROTEIN	FAT	SAT FAT	CARBS	SUGAR	FIBRE	SALT

TIKKA CHICKPEAS

If you don't have a food processor, we would really recommend you think about getting one. It makes life a lot easier and this broccoli rice possible without any hassle.

1 mug/250g **basmati rice**

1 head **broccoli**

2 tablespoons **olive oil**

2 **red onions**, sliced

400g tin **chickpeas**, rinsed and drained

½ mug/100g **macadamia nuts**

250g **chestnut mushrooms**, sliced

3 tablespoons **tikka masala curry paste**

100g **spinach**, roughly chopped

2 tablespoons freshly chopped **coriander** to serve

1 Put the rice in 2 mugs of boiling water, bring to the boil and then turn down to simmer, with a lid on the pan, for 6 minutes.

2 Remove the main stalk from the broccoli and put the florets in a food processor. Blitz until you have something resembling breadcrumbs.

3 Add the broccoli to the rice pan and replace the lid. Simmer for 4 minutes. Take off the heat, stir together, replace the lid and set to one side.

4 Meanwhile, heat the oil in a wok, or large frying pan. Add the onion and fry until the onion begins to soften.

5 Add the chickpeas, nuts and mushrooms and fry for 2 minutes.

6 Add the tikka sauce and fry for a further 2 minutes.

7 Add the spinach and coriander and stir through.

8 Serve with the broccoli rice.

RDA 100%

| 465kcal | 14g | 31g | 5g | 33g | 7g | 9g | 1g |
| CALORIES | PROTEIN | FAT | SAT FAT | CARBS | SUGAR | FIBRE | SALT |

SHIITAKE NOODLES WITH LIME BROCCOLI

Ron loves shiitake mushrooms and rightly so. They are full of flavour, compared with 'regular' mushrooms, with the addition of a flavour of 'smokiness'. We remove the stalks as they can be a little tough.

200g pack **ribbon rice noodles**

1 head **broccoli**, cut into small florets

2 tablespoons **toasted sesame oil**

1 bunch **spring onions**, sliced

1 clove **garlic**, sliced

250g **shiitake mushrooms**, stalks removed and sliced

240ml jar **hoisin sauce**

1 **fat red chilli**, chopped

1 tablespoon **toasted sesame oil**

1 tablespoon **sesame seeds**

juice of ½ **lime**

1 Put the rice noodles in a large bowl and cover with boiling water. Leave to stand for 10 minutes.

2 Put the broccoli in a pan of boiling water, simmer for 4 minutes and then drain.

3 Heat the 2 tablespoons of sesame oil in a wok and fry the onions and garlic for 1 minute.

4 Add the mushrooms and fry for 1 minute.

5 Add the hoisin sauce and chilli and heat through.

6 Add the drained noodles. Mix everything together.

7 Sprinkle the other tablespoon of sesame oil over the broccoli, along with the sesame seeds and lime juice.

8 Serve together.

RDA 100%

| 501kcal | 14g | 16g | 2g | 70g | 25g | 8g | 2g |
| CALORIES | PROTEIN | FAT | SAT FAT | CARBS | SUGAR | FIBRE | SALT |

£1.95 /PERSON · SERVES 4 · EASE ★★★★☆ · PREP 30 MINS · LEAVE 2 HOURS · GF OPTION

POLENTA TOTS WITH PORCINI MUSHROOMS

These crunchy little polenta tots are a real treat. Makes sure you take the time to fry on all sides. Dried porcini mushrooms are packed with flavour, so make sure you hold on to the cooking liquid for the end of this recipe.

GLUTEN-FREE OPTION: use GF stock.

---

1 mug/200g **coarse polenta**

3 **veg stock cubes**

4 mugs/1.2l boiling **water**

40g **dried porcini mushrooms**

4 tablespoons **olive oil**

1 **red onion**, sliced

2 cloves **garlic**, chopped

250g **mushrooms**, sliced

6 **tomatoes**, chopped

2 tablespoons **sun-dried tomato purée**

2 tablespoons freshly chopped **basil**

1   Put the polenta in a large saucepan with the stock cubes and boiling water. Simmer for about 10 minutes, stirring constantly. Season well with salt and pepper. Pour the mixture into a greased tray-bake tin and leave to set for 2 hours.

2   Meanwhile, put the porcini mushrooms in a bowl of boiling water and leave for 20 minutes. Drain, but reserve the soaking liquid. Chop and set aside.

3   Tip the polenta out of the tin and cut into 2cm chunks.

4   Put 2 tablespoons of oil in a large frying pan. Add the polenta and fry gently until all sides are browned. Set to one side.

5   Heat another 2 tablespoons of oil in a large frying pan, or wok. Add the onions and garlic and fry until the onions begin to brown. Season well.

6   Add the mushrooms and fry for 2 minutes. Add the tomatoes and fry for 2 minutes.

7   Add the rest of the ingredients, including the porcini mushrooms, and heat everything through. Add 5 tablespoons of the mushroom soaking liquid and bring to the boil.

8   Serve with the polenta tots.

RDA 100%

356kcal	7g	11g	2g	55g	8g	8g	0.5g
CALORIES	PROTEIN	FAT	SAT FAT	CARBS	SUGAR	FIBRE	SALT

TOFU WITH NEW POTATOES AND SALSA VERDE

We really do recommend organic tofu in these recipes. It is such a great ingredient and, as it is one of the main sources of 'complete' protein in a plant-based diet, it is worth getting the best possible.

GLUTEN-FREE OPTION: use GF soy sauce and GF bread.

Salsa Verde see p214

500g **new potatoes**

1 mug/180g **frozen peas**, defrosted

200g **sugar snaps**

2 x 280g packs **firm tofu**

2 tablespoons **soy sauce**

2 slices **bread**, made into breadcrumbs

zest of 2 **lemons**

½ mug/150ml **soy cream**

2 tablespoons **olive oil**

1 Make the Salsa Verde, see p214.

2 Put the potatoes in a pan of boiling water and simmer for 9 minutes. Add the peas and sugar snaps and simmer for a further 1 minute. Drain and return to the pan.

3 Meanwhile, cut the tofu into slices. Pat dry with kitchen paper. Drizzle the soy sauce over the tofu.

4 Mix together the breadcrumbs and lemon zest. Put the soy cream in a small bowl. Dip the tofu into the cream and then in the breadcrumbs.

5 Heat the oil in a large frying pan and add the tofu. Fry on each side until lightly browned.

6 Serve with the potatoes and the salsa verde.

RDA 100%

| 513kcal | 31g | 22g | 3g | 42g | 8g | 10g | 3g |
| CALORIES | PROTEIN | FAT | SAT FAT | CARBS | SUGAR | FIBRE | SALT |

MUSHROOMS AND GARLIC CRISPS ON A CAULIFLOWER PURÉE

This meal is a lovely, delicate dish, so cooking it correctly is important. Take care to not burn the garlic crisps when frying them. Just keep your eye on them and remove from the pan as soon as they are done.

GLUTEN-FREE OPTION: use GF soy sauce.

2 medium **cauliflowers**

3 tablespoons **cashew cream**

3 tablespoons **olive oil**

4 cloves **garlic**, sliced

500g **chestnut mushrooms**, sliced

1 tablespoon **soy sauce**

200g **spinach**

1 Break up the cauliflower into florets. Put in a pan of boiling, salted water and simmer for 5 minutes.

2 Drain and return to the pan. Add the cashew cream and blend with a hand-held blender. Season with salt and pepper and set to one side until needed.

3 Heat the oil in a large frying pan, or wok. Fry the garlic on a medium heat until lightly browned, taking care not to burn it. Remove from the pan and set to one side until needed.

4 Add the mushrooms and fry for 3–4 minutes until they begin to brown lightly. Season well.

5 Add the soy and spinach and heat until the spinach wilts.

6 Serve with the garlic crisps sprinkled on top.

RDA 100%

352kcal	10g	17g	3g	11g	5g	5g	1g
CALORIES	PROTEIN	FAT	SAT FAT	CARBS	SUGAR	FIBRE	SALT

EDAMAME BEAN PASTA

This is a great 'raid of the store-cupboard' meal, with only a few fresh ingredients needed. Also good for when you are waiting for payday.

GLUTEN-FREE OPTION: use GF pasta, soy sauce and stock.

---

3 mugs/500g **pasta**

2 tablespoons **rapeseed oil**

2 **onions**, chopped

2 cloves **garlic**, chopped

1 **fat red chilli**, chopped

6 **tomatoes**, chopped

SAUCE

1 tablespoon **cornflour**

³/₄ mug/225ml **water**

6 tablespoons **peanut butter**

1 tablespoon **soy sauce**

1 **veg stock cube**

3 mugs/480g **frozen edamame beans,** defrosted

bunch **spring onions,** chopped

1 Put the pasta in a large pan of boiling, salted water and simmer for 10 minutes. Drain and return to the pan.

2 Meanwhile, heat the oil in a large saucepan and add the onions, garlic and chilli. Fry for 2–3 minutes until the onion begins to soften.

3 Add the tomatoes and fry for another 2 minutes.

4 Mix together the sauce ingredients and add to the pan containing the onions. Season and bring to the boil. Blitz with a blender until smooth.

5 Add the edamame beans, spring onions and pasta to the sauce and mix.

RDA 100%

839kcal	33g	42g	5g	87g	15g	15g	1g
CALORIES	PROTEIN	FAT	SAT FAT	CARBS	SUGAR	FIBRE	SALT

PUTTANESCA

The cherry tomatoes, black olives and basil combine in this recipe to make a wonderful, fresh, Mediterranean-style meal. Ideal for when you don't have much time.

GLUTEN-FREE OPTION: use GF pasta.

---

3 mugs/300g **penne**

2 tablespoons **olive oil**

1 **red onion**, chopped

4 cloves of **garlic**, chopped

2 **fat red chillies**, chopped

300g **cherry tomatoes**, chopped

½ mug/150ml **water**

20 **black olives**, chopped

2 tablespoons **capers**, chopped

2 tablespoons **sun-dried tomato purée**

2 tablespoons freshly chopped **basil**

1 Put the penne in a pan of boiling, salted water and simmer for 10 minutes. Drain and return to the pan.

2 Meanwhile, heat the oil in a large frying pan and add the onions, garlic and chillies. Fry until the onion begins to soften.

3 Add the rest of the ingredients, apart from the basil, and simmer for 2 minutes.

4 Stir in the basil and cooked penne.

RDA 100%

253kcal	5g	11g	2g	35g	6g	3g	1g
CALORIES	PROTEIN	FAT	SAT FAT	CARBS	SUGAR	FIBRE	SALT

GREENS RISOTTO

WHERE ON EARTH: nutritional yeast, can be bought online at places like Healthy Supplies and Amazon. It is a great source of vitamin B12.

GLUTEN-FREE OPTION: use GF stock.

½ mug/100g **cashew nuts**

2 tablespoons **olive oil**

1 **red onion**, sliced

2 cloves **garlic**, chopped

1 mug/250g **basmati rice**

10 pieces **sun-dried tomatoes**, chopped

3 tablespoons **nutritional yeast**

2 mugs/600ml **water** + 1 **veg stock cube**

100g **green beans**, halved

200g **kale**

25g freshly chopped **basil**

1. Put the cashews in a wok and dry-fry for 2 minutes, taking care not to burn them. Remove from the pan and set to one side.

2. Add the oil to the pan, along with the onions and garlic, and fry for 2 minutes.

3. Add the rice and fry for 1 minute. Add the sun-dried tomatoes, nutritional yeast, water and stock cube and season well. Simmer for 5 minutes, with a lid on the pan.

4. Add the green beans and kale, but don't stir. Put the lid back on the pan and continue to simmer for another 5 minutes.

5. Add the basil and stir everything together.

RDA 100%

| 367kcal | 14g | 25g | 4g | 26g | 7g | 8g | 1g |
| CALORIES | PROTEIN | FAT | SAT FAT | CARBS | SUGAR | FIBRE | SALT |

MEXICAN RICE

This is quite a mild dish. If you like your food to 'blow your head off', then just keep adding those chillies.

GLUTEN-FREE OPTION: use GF stock.

2 tablespoons **rapeseed oil**

1 **onion**, chopped

2 cloves **garlic**, chopped

1 ½ mugs/375g **basmati rice**

6 **tomatoes**, chopped

3 tablespoons **tomato purée**

400g **black beans**

2 teaspoons **smoked paprika**

2 teaspoons **cumin**

1 **fat red chilli**, chopped

1 teaspoon **coconut sugar**

3 mugs/900ml **water**

1 **veg stock cube**

SAUCE

4 tablespoons **cashew butter**, see p211

²/₃ mug/200ml **almond milk**

3 tablespoons **nutritional yeast**

1 tablespoon **miso paste**

juice of ½ **lemon**

1 Heat the oil in a large frying pan, add the onion and garlic and fry for 2 minutes.

2 Add the rice, season and fry for 1 minute.

3 Add the tomatoes and fry for 2 minutes.

4 Add the rest of the ingredients and bring to the boil. Turn down to simmer, with a lid on the pan, for 10 minutes.

5 Meanwhile, put the sauce ingredients in a small pan and bring to the boil. Simmer for 1 minute.

6 Serve the rice with the sauce drizzled over.

RDA 100%

495kcal	20g	26g	4g	52g	13g	10g	1g
CALORIES	PROTEIN	FAT	SAT FAT	CARBS	SUGAR	FIBRE	SALT

JACKFRUIT TERYAKI

We got confused with our origins here. The sweet and sour is definitely Chinese while the jackfruit is more Indian. If, like many on a Friday night, you can't decide between Chinese or Indian, why not have both? Just eat your Indian dish with chopsticks, like us.

WHERE ON EARTH: jackfruit can be found with the canned vegetables.

GLUTEN-FREE OPTION: use GF soy sauce.

SAUCE

100g **cashew butter**

4 tablespoons **olive oil**

½ mug/150ml **almond milk**

1 tablespoon **cider vinegar**

3 tablespoons **maple syrup**

3 tablespoons **soy sauce**

1 tablespoon **mirin**

½ mug/150ml **water**

1 ½ mugs/375g **basmati rice**

2 tablespoons **coconut oil**

1 **onion**, sliced

2 cloves **garlic**, chopped

400g tin **jackfruit**, roughly chopped

250g **mushrooms**

1 tablespoon **sesame seeds**

1 tablespoon freshly chopped **coriander**, to serve

1 Mix the sauce ingredients together in a small pan and bring to the boil. Set to one side until needed.

2 Put the rice in a saucepan with 3 mugs of boiling water. Bring to the boil and then turn down to simmer, with a lid on the pan, for 10 minutes.

3 Meanwhile, heat the coconut oil in a large frying pan. Add the onions and garlic and fry for 2 minutes.

4 Add the jackfruit and fry for 2 minutes.

5 Add the mushrooms and fry for 2 minutes.

6 Add the sauce and simmer for 5 minutes.

7 Serve with the rice and sprinkle with sesame seeds and coriander.

RDA 100%

571kcal	13g	39g	12g	49g	11g	7g	3g
CALORIES	PROTEIN	FAT	SAT FAT	CARBS	SUGAR	FIBRE	SALT

ASPARAGUS RISOTTO

Joy cheats when making her risottos. Instead of standing over a pan, stirring it for 20 minutes to get all the starch out of risotto rice, she uses basmati rice and adds some soy cream at the end. Et, voilà! Super-speedy risotto!

GLUTEN-FREE OPTION: use GF stock.

---

2 tablespoons **rapeseed oil**

2 **leeks**, sliced

1 ½ mugs/375g **basmati rice**

3 mugs/900ml **water**

2 **veg stock cubes**

250g **asparagus**

1 mug/160g **frozen edamame beans**, defrosted

1 **courgette**, cut into small chunks

1 tablespoon freshly chopped **mint**

1 tablespoon freshly chopped **parsley**

juice of a **lemon**

⅓ mug/100ml **soy cream**

4 tablespoons **flaked almonds**

1 Heat the oil in a large frying pan, or wok. Add the leeks and fry until they begin soften.

2 Add the rice and cook for 1 minute.

3 Add the water and stock cubes and bring to the boil. Season well with salt and pepper. Turn down to simmer, with a lid on the pan, for 5 minutes.

4 Cut the asparagus stalks into small rings, leaving the tips until later. Add the stalks to the risotto and simmer for 5 minutes.

5 Add the edamame beans, asparagus tips and courgette. Stir and simmer for a further 5 minutes.

6 Add the mint, parsley, lemon juice and soy cream. Mix together and heat through.

7 Serve with the almonds on top.

RDA 100%

298kcal	13g	16g	2g	30g	6g	4g	0.1g
CALORIES	PROTEIN	FAT	SAT FAT	CARBS	SUGAR	FIBRE	SALT

£1.59 /PERSON · SERVES 4 · EASE ★★★★☆ · PREP 20 MINS · COOK 25 MINS · GF OPTION

SAVOY CABBAGE BALLS

We know that 'Savoy Cabbage Balls' sounds bizarre, but trust us, they really work.

GLUTEN-FREE OPTION: use GF flour and soy sauce.

BALLS

½ **savoy cabbage**

1 **carrot**

½ mug/100g **cashews**

1 **red pepper**

bunch **spring onions**, finely chopped

¼ teaspoon **black pepper**

½ teaspoon **salt**

200g **vegan cream cheese**

2 tablespoons **flour**

1 ½ mugs/375g **basmati rice**

SAUCE

1 tablespoon **oil**

bunch **spring onions**, chopped

1 **fat red chilli**, chopped

1 tablespoon freshly grated **ginger**

1 ½ mugs/450ml **water**

2 tablespoons **soy sauce**

1 tablespoon **cider vinegar**

1 tablespoon **maple syrup**

1 ½ tablespoons **cornflour**

1 Preheat the oven to 200°C fan oven/220°C/gas 7. Grease or line a baking tray.

2 Put the coarse grater blade on the food processor and put the cabbage, carrot, nuts, and pepper through. Put into a bowl and mix in the rest of the veggie ball ingredients. Add more flour if they are too sticky to roll into balls.

3 Make into 24 balls (flouring your hands if necessary) and place on the baking tray.

4 Bake in the oven for 25 minutes.

5 Meanwhile, put the rice in a saucepan with 3 mugs of boiling water. Bring to the boil and then turn down to simmer, with a lid on the pan, for 10 minutes.

6 To make the sauce, heat the oil in a saucepan and add the onions, chilli and ginger. Fry for 1 minute.

7 Add the rest of the sauce ingredients to the saucepan and bring to the boil. The sauce will thicken.

RDA 100%

415kcal	10g	28g	13g	27g	14g	5g	2g
CALORIES	PROTEIN	FAT	SAT FAT	CARBS	SUGAR	FIBRE	SALT

TOMATO AND FENNEL CASSEROLE

Not your 'regular' casserole. This packs a big punch of flavour with the lemon and fennel, along with the fragrance of the rosemary.

WHERE ON EARTH: harrissa paste is normally with the spices.

GLUTEN-FREE OPTION: use GF stock.

---

4 medium **potatoes**, cut into 2cm chunks

2 tablespoons **olive oil**

CASSEROLE

2 tablespoons **olive oil**

1 **fennel bulb**, cut into thin slices

2 **red onions**, sliced

6 **tomatoes**, chopped

400g tin **cannellini beans**

3 tablespoons **tomato purée**

1 mug/300ml **water**

2 **veg stock cubes**

1 tablespoon **harissa paste**

1 **lemon**, cut into 4

1 tablespoon fresh **rosemary**, chopped

broccoli, cut into florets

1 Preheat the oven to 180°C fan oven/200°C/gas 6.

2 Put the potatoes on a roasting tray and drizzle over the oil. Season with salt and pepper, mix everything together and then spread out evenly. Roast in the oven for 50 minutes.

3 Heat the oil in a hob-to-oven casserole dish. Add the fennel and onions and fry for 3–4 minutes until things start to brown.

4 Add the rest of the casserole ingredients and bring to the boil. Season well with salt and pepper.

5 Roast in the oven, with no lid on the pan, for 30 minutes, or until the roast potatoes begin to brown.

6 5 minutes before the end of the cooking time, put the broccoli in a pan of boiling, salted water. Simmer for 5 minutes and then drain. Serve.

RDA 100%

669kcal	14g	17g	3g	47g	15g	12g	0.2g
CALORIES	PROTEIN	FAT	SAT FAT	CARBS	SUGAR	FIBRE	SALT

LEEK AND POTATO GRATIN

This works just as well in a single casserole dish, but if you have got some small dishes, like ours, it's a fun way to present food, especially when friends come over.

If you don't eat all the pickled beetroot in one go, it will keep for a month or so in the fridge.

GLUTEN-FREE OPTION: use GF bread.

---

3 medium **potatoes**, peeled and cut into 2cm chunks

2 teaspoons **Dijon mustard**

200g **vegan cream cheese**

30g **vegan margarine (Tomor)**

2 **leeks**, sliced

2 tablespoons freshly chopped **chives**

1 slice of **bread**, made into breadcrumbs

½ mug/100g **peanuts**

1 tablespoon **olive oil**

beetroot pickle, see p208

1 Preheat the oven to 180°C fan oven/200°C/gas 6.

2 Put the potatoes in a small saucepan of boiling water. Bring to the boil and simmer, with a lid on the pan, for 8 minutes. Drain and return to the pan, add the mustard and cream cheese and then mash. Season well with salt and pepper.

3 Heat the margarine in a large frying pan and add the leeks. Fry until they begin to soften and brown.

4 Take off the heat, add the chives and potatoes, and mix together.

5 Divide the mixture between the 4 ramekins.

6 Put the bread and peanuts in a food processor and blitz. Add the tablespoon of oil and pulse a few times. Divide between the ramekins.

7 Place on the roasting tray and bake in the oven for 25 minutes.

8 Serve with the pickled beetroot.

RDA 100%

| 520kcal | 14g | 34g | 16g | 35g | 9g | 5g | 2g |
| CALORIES | PROTEIN | FAT | SAT FAT | CARBS | SUGAR | FIBRE | SALT |

LENTIL DHAL

This is one of Ben's favourites from the book. He a sucker for a lentil curry. Add to that, cashews, which he seems to be constantly snacking on from the NOSH Larder, and it's a winner!

GLUTEN-FREE OPTION: use GF stock.

1 ½ mugs/375g **basmati rice**

2 tablespoons **coconut oil**

1 **onion**, chopped

2 cloves **garlic**, chopped

2 tablespoons freshly grated **ginger**

2 teaspoons **cumin**

2 teaspoons **garam masala**

1 teaspoon **turmeric**

1 **fat red chilli**, chopped

1 tablespoon **coconut sugar**

½ mug/150ml **water +**
1 **veg stock cube**

6 **tomatoes**, chopped

2 x 400g tins **green lentils**, rinsed and drained

400ml tin **coconut milk**

½ mug/100g **cashews**

2 tablespoons freshly chopped **coriander** to serve

1   Put the rice in a saucepan with 3 mugs of boiling water. Bring to the boil and then turn down to simmer, with a lid on the pan, for 10 minutes.

2   Heat the oil in a wok, or large frying pan. Add the onions and garlic and fry for 2 minutes.

3   Add the ginger, cumin, garam masala, turmeric and chilli. Fry for a further 2 minutes and season well.

4   Add the rest of the ingredients and simmer gently for 5 minutes.

5   Serve with the rice, and garnish with coriander.

RDA 100%

595kcal	17g	36g	22g	54g	14g	11g	0.2g
CALORIES	PROTEIN	FAT	SAT FAT	CARBS	SUGAR	FIBRE	SALT

MOUSSAKA

GLUTEN-FREE OPTION: use GF flour.

---

4 tablespoons **plain flour**

1 teaspoon **allspice**

¼ teaspoon **nutmeg**

¼ teaspoon **ground ginger**

½ teaspoon **cinnamon**

2 **aubergines**, cut into 2cm slices

2 tablespoons **olive oil**

SAUCE

2 tablespoons **olive oil**

1 **onion**, chopped

2 cloves **garlic**, chopped

6 **tomatoes**, chopped

6 pieces **sun-dried tomatoes**, chopped

2 tablespoons **tomato purée**

1 tablespoon **pomegranate molasses**

juice of a **lemon**

2 **courgettes**, sliced

100g **cooked, green lentils**

2 x 400g tins **black chickpeas**

½ mug/150ml **water**

SALAD

Romaine lettuce, sliced

½ **cucumber**, diced

1 bunch **spring onions**, chopped

200g **cherry tomatoes**, halved

DRESSING

juice of a **lemon**

2 tablespoons extra virgin **olive oil**

1 tablespoon **maple syrup**

salt and **pepper**

1 Preheat the oven to 180°C fan oven/200°C/gas 6. Grease a medium-sized casserole dish and roasting tray.

2 Mix the flour and spices together and dip the sliced aubergines in the mixture. Place on the roasting tray, drizzle with oil and roast in the oven for 10 minutes. After 10 minutes, turn them over and return to the oven for a further 10 minutes.

3 Meanwhile, make the sauce. Heat the oil in a large frying pan and add the onions and garlic. Fry until the onions begin to brown.

4 Add the tomatoes and fry for 4 minutes.

5 Add the rest of the sauce ingredients and season well with salt and pepper. Simmer for 5 minutes.

6 Put half the sauce in a large casserole dish. Add the aubergines and then the rest of the sauce on top.

7 Bake in the oven for 30 minutes.

8 Serve with the salad and combined dressing ingredients.

RDA 100%

132

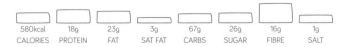

580kcal	18g	23g	3g	67g	26g	16g	1g
CALORIES	PROTEIN	FAT	SAT FAT	CARBS	SUGAR	FIBRE	SALT

£ 1.79 /PERSON · SERVES 4 · EASE ★★☆☆☆ · PREP 20 MINS · GF OPTION

CARBONARA

If you are new to being a vegan, and struggling to cook without eggs, here's a little concoction of ingredients to prove you don't need eggs any more.

GLUTEN-FREE OPTION: use GF spaghetti and soy sauce.

280g **firm tofu**, diced small

250g **chestnut mushrooms**, chopped

5 tablespoons **soy sauce**

1 tablespoon **maple syrup**

1 tablespoon **cider vinegar**

300g **spaghetti**

2 mugs/360g **frozen peas**, defrosted

1 tablespoon **rapeseed oil**

1 **red onion**, chopped

100g **cashew butter**

1 tablespoon **nutritional yeast**

⅓ mug/200ml **almond milk**

2 tablespoons **coconut crisps**, (optional) see p212

2 tablespoons freshly chopped **parsley**

1 Mix the tofu, mushrooms, soy sauce, maple syrup and cider vinegar in a large bowl and leave to marinate for 5 minutes.

2 Put the spaghetti in a large saucepan of boiling water and simmer for 8 minutes. Add the peas and simmer for a further 2 minutes. Drain, reserving some of the cooking liquid.

3 Meanwhile, heat the oil in a wok and fry the onions until they begin to soften.

4 Add the tofu mix to the wok and bring to the boil. Simmer for 2 minutes.

5 Mix together the cashew butter, yeast and milk until smooth and add to the pan.

6 Stir in the spaghetti and peas and add a little of the cooking liquid from the spaghetti.

7 Serve with the coconut crisps and parsley.

RDA 100%

| 743kcal | 32g | 31g | 9g | 79g | 7g | 11g | 4g |
| CALORIES | PROTEIN | FAT | SAT FAT | CARBS | SUGAR | FIBRE | SALT |

£ 1.74 /PERSON · **SERVES 4** · **EASE ★★★☆☆** · **PREP 25 MINS** · **COOK 30 MINS** · **GF OPTION**

PASTA CAPONATA

Although this says 25mins prep and 30mins in the oven, you should have your food on the table in about 40 minutes. You'll do some of the prep while the oven is doing its job.

GLUTEN-FREE OPTION: use GF pasta.

2 **aubergines**, cut into 2cm dice

400g **cherry tomatoes**

1 **fat red chilli**, chopped

3 tablespoons **olive oil**

1 **red onion**, roughly chopped

2 sticks **celery**, chopped

3 mugs/300g **penne**

SAUCE

1 mug/300ml **water**

2 teaspoons **cornflour**

3 tablespoons **sun-dried tomato purée**

2 tablespoons freshly chopped **basil**

¼ mug/40g **raisins**

20 **black olives**

2 tablespoons **coconut sugar**

1 tablespoon **balsamic vinegar**

½ mug/75g **pine nuts**

1 Preheat the oven to 200°C fan oven/220°C/ gas 7.

2 Put the aubergines, tomatoes, chilli, olive oil, onion and celery on a large roasting tray. Season well with salt and pepper and mix everything together. Spread out and roast in the oven for 30 minutes.

3 15 minutes before the end of the cooking time, put the penne in a large pan of boiling, salted water. Simmer for 10 minutes.

4 Meanwhile, mix the sauce ingredients together in a large jug.

5 Drain the cooked penne and leave in the colander. Add the sauce ingredients to the penne pan and bring to the boil, the sauce should thicken a little. Simmer for 1 minute.

6 Add the penne to the saucepan and mix.

7 Take the veggies out of the oven and add to the pan. Stir together.

8 Serve with the pine nuts sprinkled over the top.

RDA 100%

340kcal	11g	26g	3g	63g	18g	7g	1g
CALORIES	PROTEIN	FAT	SAT FAT	CARBS	SUGAR	FIBRE	SALT

MUSHROOM PHO

Traditionally a 'Pho' is a broth. Our Mushroom Pho is slightly less broth-like, but is a delightfully fresh noodle dish, with a hint of spice.

GLUTEN-FREE OPTION: use GF soy sauce.

200g **rice noodles**

2 tablespoons **toasted sesame oil**

1 **onion**, thinly sliced

4 cloves **garlic**, chopped

2 tablespoons freshly grated **ginger**

1 **fat red chilli** sliced

500g **shiitake mushrooms**, sliced

juice of 2 **oranges**

2 tablespoons **tamarind paste**

4 tablespoons **soy sauce**

4 tablespoons **maple syrup**

½ mug/150ml **water**

300g **fresh bean sprouts**

2 **pak choi**, sliced

2 tablespoons freshly chopped **coriander**

2 tablespoons freshly chopped **mint**

1   Put the rice noodles in a bowl of boiling water. Leave to stand for 10 minutes and then drain.

2   Meanwhile, heat the oil in a wok. Add the onions and garlic and fry until they begin to soften.

3   Add the ginger, chilli and mushrooms and fry for 1 minute.

4   Add the rest of the ingredients and bring to the boil. Serve.

RDA 100%

| 479kcal | 16g | 13g | 2g | 69g | 21g | 11g | 3g |
| CALORIES | PROTEIN | FAT | SAT FAT | CARBS | SUGAR | FIBRE | SALT |

£3.33 /PERSON  SERVES 4 EASE ★★★☆☆ PREP 35 MINS GF

FENNEL TAGINE WITH POMEGRANATE SALSA

WHERE ON EARTH: pomegranate seeds are in the 'salad' section of the 'Fruit and Veg' area.

6 **tomatoes**

100g **medjool dates**, stoned

2 **cinnamon sticks**

2 teaspoons **coriander**

1 teaspoon **turmeric**

2 tablespoons **rapeseed oil**

1 **onion**, chopped

2 tablespoons freshly grated **ginger**

3 cloves **garlic**, chopped

2 **fennel** bulbs, sliced

1 **celeriac**, cut into 2cm cubes

1 **fat red chilli**, sliced

150g **spinach**

POMEGRANATE SALSA

250g **pomegranate seeds**

2 **spring onions**, chopped

juice of a **lime**

2 tablespoons freshly chopped **mint**

3 tablespoons **extra virgin olive oil**

1 large **cauliflower**

1 tablespoon rapeseed **oil**

2 tablespoons freshly chopped **coriander**

1 Put the tomatoes and medjool dates in a blender and blitz until smooth.

2 Dry fry the cinnamon sticks, coriander and turmeric in a large frying pan for 1 minute.

3 Add the oil, onion, ginger and garlic and fry for 1 minute. Season with salt and pepper.

4 Add the tomato paste, fennel, and celeriac. Bring to the boil and simmer for 25 minutes.

5 Mix together the salsa ingredients.

6 Cut the cauliflower into florets and put in a food processor. Blitz until it resembles breadcrumbs.

7 Heat the oil in a large frying pan and add the cauliflower. Fry on a medium heat, stirring frequently, until the cauliflower begins to steam. Take off the heat and add the coriander.

8 Add the chilli and spinach to the tagine and simmer for 1 minute.

9 Serve with the couscous and the salsa.

RDA 100%

477kcal	9g	23g	3g	45g	37g	15g	1g
CALORIES	PROTEIN	FAT	SAT FAT	CARBS	SUGAR	FIBRE	SALT

£2.09 /PERSON · SERVES 4 · EASE ★★★★★ · PREP 30 MINS · COOK 35 MINS · GF OPTION

BEAN AND APPLE EN CROUTE

WHERE ON EARTH: flax seeds and vegetable suet are in the 'Baking' section.

GLUTEN-FREE OPTION: use vegan GF pastry, bread, and soy sauce.

FILLING

1 tablespoon **flax seeds**

3 tablespoons **water**

½ **onion**

2 cloves **garlic**

1 slice **white bread**

1 **Granny Smith apple**, cored

150g **mushrooms**

1 tablespoon **soy sauce**

200g **pinto beans**

½ mug/75g **peanuts**

50g **vegetable suet**

1 tablespoon chopped **chives**

1 sheet **ready-rolled vegan puff pastry**

soy cream to brush

SALAD

2 **pink grapefruits**, peeled and sliced

1 **Romaine lettuce**, thinly sliced

½ **cucumber** cubed

140g **chicory**, thinly sliced

2 tablespoons **maple syrup**

2 tablespoons **olive oil**

1 Preheat the oven to 180°C fan oven/200°C/gas 6. Grease a large baking tray.

2 Put the flax seeds in a small bowl with the water and leave to stand for 10 minutes.

3 Put the onion, garlic, bread and apple in a food processor and blitz until you have something resembling breadcrumbs. Add the rest of the filling ingredients, including the flax seeds. Season well, and pulse a few times, until things hold together.

4 Unroll the pastry and put the mixture along one side of the pastry. There may be a bit extra filling - just form it into shapes and cook alongside the rolls. Wet one edge of the pastry and flip it over. Trim to form the long roll. Place on the baking sheet, brush with soy cream and bake in the oven for 35 minutes.

5 Mix together the salad ingredients and serve.

RDA 100%

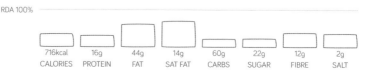

| 716kcal | 16g | 44g | 14g | 60g | 22g | 12g | 2g |
| CALORIES | PROTEIN | FAT | SAT FAT | CARBS | SUGAR | FIBRE | SALT |

THAI AUBERGINE CURRY

This is an absolute favourite in Tim's family…because it's quick and…it tastes good!

GLUTEN-FREE OPTION: use GF soy sauce.

---

2 tablespoons **olive oil**

1 **onion**, sliced

1 **fat red chilli**, chopped

3 tablespoons **vegan Thai green curry paste**

⅓ mug/100ml **coconut milk**

3 tablespoons **soy sauce**

1 tablespoon **coconut sugar**

1 large **aubergine**, cut into strips

225g tin **bamboo shoots**, drained

200g **green beans**

3 **lime leaves**

1½ mugs/375g **basmati rice**

1. Heat the oil in a wok, or large frying pan. Add the onion and chilli and fry until they begin to brown.

2. Add the curry paste, coconut milk, soy sauce and sugar and bring to the boil.

3. Add the aubergine, bamboo shoots, beans and lime leaves. Simmer for 10 minutes.

4. Put the rice in a saucepan with 3 mugs of boiling water. Bring to the boil and then turn down to simmer, with a lid on the pan, for 10 minutes.

5. Serve the rice, with the curry on top.

RDA 100%

281kcal	7g	17g	5g	33g	10g	5g	3g
CALORIES	PROTEIN	FAT	SAT FAT	CARBS	SUGAR	FIBRE	SALT

MUSHROOM STROGANOFF

Creamy, rich and packed with savoury flavour from the combination of nuts, mushrooms and nutritional yeast.

WHERE ON EARTH: nutritional yeast is difficult to find in supermakets, so we buy ours from Healthy Supplies, online.

GLUTEN-FREE OPTION: use GF stock and soy sauce.

---

1 ½ mugs/375g **basmati rice**

½ teaspoon **turmeric**

2 tablespoons **olive oil**

½ mug/100g **cashews**

1 **onion**, chopped

2 cloves **garlic**, chopped

500g **chestnut mushrooms**, sliced

1 tablespoon **soy sauce**

1 **veg stock cube** +
½ mug/150ml **water**

1 ½ tablespoons **nutritional yeast**

25g freshly chopped **parsley**

⅔ mug/200ml **soy cream**

1 tablespoon **wholegrain mustard**

1   Put the rice in a saucepan with 3 mugs of water and the turmeric. Bring to the boil and then simmer, with a lid on the pan, for 10 minutes.

2   Meanwhile, heat the oil in a wok, or large frying pan. Add the cashews, onions and garlic and fry for 2 minutes.

3   Add the mushrooms and fry for 2 minutes. Season with salt and pepper.

4   Add the rest of the ingredients and bring to the boil. Turn down to simmer for 2 minutes.

5   Serve with the rice.

RDA 100%

357kcal	13g	23g	4g	33g	6g	5g	2g
CALORIES	PROTEIN	FAT	SAT FAT	CARBS	SUGAR	FIBRE	SALT

£1.38 /PERSON — SERVES 4 — EASE ★★★☆☆ — PREP 25MINS — GF OPTION

SQUASH AND SPINACH CURRY

This recipe can pack a real punch if you want it to. It really depends on the type of chilli you use and whether you remove the seeds or not.

GLUTEN-FREE OPTION: use GF stock.

2 tablespoons **rapeseed oil**

1 **onion**, chopped

2 cloves **garlic**, chopped

2 tablespoons freshly grated **ginger**

1 **fat red chilli**, chopped

1 teaspoon **turmeric**

1 teaspoon **ground coriander**

1 teaspoon **cumin**

1 teaspoon **garam masala**

500g **butternut squash**, peeled and cut into 2cm chunks

400g tin **chickpeas**, rinsed and drained

400ml tin **coconut milk**

1 **veg stock cube**

200g **spinach**

1 large **cauliflower**

2 tablespoons **rapeseed oil**

1 Heat the oil in a wok, or large frying pan. Add the onion, garlic, ginger and chilli and fry until the onions begin to soften.

2 Add the spices and fry for 2 minutes, stirring frequently.

3 Add the squash and chickpeas and fry for 2 minutes. Season with salt and pepper.

4 Add the coconut milk and stock cube and bring to the boil. Simmer for 10 minutes.

5 Add the spinach and heat until it wilts.

6 Cut the cauliflower into florets, place in a food processor and blitz. Don't make it too fine.

7 Heat the oil in a large frying pan and add the cauliflower. Cook for 2–3 minutes. Once it begins to 'steam', it is ready. Serve with the curry.

RDA 100%

341kcal	11g	18g	12g	31g	13g	8g	0.3g
CALORIES	PROTEIN	FAT	SAT FAT	CARBS	SUGAR	FIBRE	SALT

CHESTNUT AND TOFU ROAST

Here is an interesting twist to a nut roast, with avocado and tofu as a topping. It is also packed with energy, good fat and protein from all the nuts.

GLUTEN-FREE OPTION: use GF stock.

1 **onion**, peeled and quartered
1 mug/200g **hazelnuts**
1 mug/200g **cashew nuts**
1 slice **bread**
1 **veg stock cube**
²/₃ mug/200ml **hot water**
2 tablespoons **coconut oil**
100g **whole, cooked chestnuts**
1 tablespoon freshly chopped **basil**

TOPPING
300g **silken tofu**
1 **avocado**, cubed
250g **chestnut mushrooms**, sliced

SALAD
1 **Little Gem lettuce**
1 bunch **spring onions**, sliced
1 **fennel bulb**, sliced
2 **oranges**, peeled and sliced
¹/₂ mug/50g **flaked almonds**
2 tablespoons **olive oil**

1 Preheat the oven to 180°C fan oven/200°C/gas 6. Grease a small casserole dish.

2 Put the onion, hazelnuts, cashews, chestnuts and bread in a food processor and blitz until you have something resembling breadcrumbs.

3 Mix the stock cube and coconut oil into the hot water and add to the processor, with the chestnuts and basil. Season with salt and pepper and pulse a couple of times. Turn out into the casserole dish.

4 Mix the tofu to a smooth paste. Add the avocado and mushrooms, mix together and spread over the top of the nut mixture. Bake in the oven for 50 minutes.

5 Mix together the salad ingredients and season well with salt and pepper.

6 Serve with the nut roast.

RDA 100%

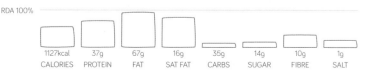

1127kcal	37g	67g	16g	35g	14g	10g	1g
CALORIES	PROTEIN	FAT	SAT FAT	CARBS	SUGAR	FIBRE	SALT

ROASTED SPICED TOFU WITH POTATO ROSTI

Roasting tofu makes it easy to get a crispy coating around each piece and therefore increasing the surface area for flavour. By the way, if you have never made potato rosti before, you are missing out! A simple way to make potatoes taste amazing!

280g **firm tofu**

300g **cherry tomatoes**

1 teaspoon **chilli powder**

1 teaspoon **paprika**

1 teaspoon **cumin**

1 teaspoon **coriander**

2 tablespoons **olive oil**

CORIANDER CREAM

200g **vegan cream cheese**

juice of a **lime**

bunch **spring onions**

2 tablespoons fresh **coriander**

4 medium **potatoes**, grated

2 tablespoons olive **oil**

chilli jam, (optional) see p216

1 Preheat the oven to 180°C fan oven/200°C/gas 6.

2 Cut the tofu into chunks and place on a large roasting tray with the cherry tomatoes. Sprinkle with the chilli powder, paprika, cumin and coriander and drizzle over with oil. Season with salt and pepper. Mix everything together and then spread things out evenly. Roast in the oven for 30 minutes.

3 Meanwhile, put the soft cheese, lime juice, spring onions and coriander in a food processor and blitz to a smooth paste. Season well with salt and pepper and set to one side until needed.

4 To make the rosti, heat the oil in a large frying pan. Take small handfuls of the grated potato (divide the mixture into 8, as you will need to cook them in batches) and put them in the frying pan. Fry on a medium heat until the potatoes are browned underneath. Season with salt and pepper. Turn over and fry on the other side until browned.

5 Serve with the roasted tofu, tomatoes, coriander cream and chilli jam.

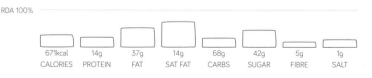

RDA 100%

671kcal	14g	37g	14g	68g	42g	5g	1g
CALORIES	PROTEIN	FAT	SAT FAT	CARBS	SUGAR	FIBRE	SALT

SOY BEAN AND PEANUT HOT POT

Don't worry if the sauce bubbles up and goes all over the potatoes (like ours did). Just claim it was all part of the plan to increase flavour.

GLUTEN-FREE OPTION: use GF stock, flour and soy sauce.

2 tablespoons **olive oil**

2 **onions**, sliced

2 cloves **garlic**, chopped

½ mug/100g **peanuts**

1 tablespoon **flour**

2 mugs/600ml **water**

2 **veg stock cubes**

6 **tomatoes**, chopped

3 tablespoons **tomato purée**

3 **carrots**, sliced

3 mugs/480g **frozen soy beans,** defrosted

3 tablespoons **soy sauce**

5 medium **potatoes**, sliced

1 Heat the oil in a large hob-to-oven casserole dish. Add the onion and garlic and fry for 2 minutes.

2 Add the peanuts and fry for 2 minutes.

3 Add the flour and mix well.

4 Add the rest of the ingredients, apart from the potato, season well and bring to the boil.

5 Arrange the sliced potatoes on the top of the hot pot (see photo). Season with salt and pepper.

6 Put a lid on the pan and bake in the oven for 25 minutes.

7 Take the lid off the pan and bake for another 35 minutes, or until the potatoes are nicely browned and crunchy.

RDA 100%

646kcal	30g	26g	4g	65g	24g	17g	2g
CALORIES	PROTEIN	FAT	SAT FAT	CARBS	SUGAR	FIBRE	SALT

ROAST FENNEL ON SPINACH WITH PEA PURÉE

Roasting fennel mellows the strong aniseed flavour and turns it quite sweet. Twin that with the chilli jam and you have a winner.

2 whole **fennel**

3 tablespoons **olive oil**

1 tablespoon **balsamic vinegar**

5 medium **potatoes**, cut into 2cm chunks

2 tablespoons **olive oil**

2 mugs/360g **frozen peas**, defrosted

25g **vegan margarine (Tomor)**

200g **spinach**

chilli jam, see p216

1 Preheat the oven to 180°C fan oven/200°C/gas 6.

2 Cut each fennel bulb, from root to top, into 4 pieces. Lay the pieces on a greased casserole dish and drizzle with oil and balsamic. Season and roast in the oven for 45–50 minutes.

3 Put the potatoes on a roasting tray, drizzle over the oil and season well with salt and pepper. Mix together and then spread the pieces out. Roast in the oven for 45 minutes.

4 5 minutes before the end of the roasting time, put the peas in a pan of boiling water and simmer for 1 minute.

5 Drain and return the peas to the pan with the margarine and chopped spinach. Put a lid on the pan and heat for 30 seconds.

6 Season well with salt and pepper and blitz together with a blender.

7 Serve with chilli jam.

RDA 100%

678kcal	17g	26g	5g	82g	43g	15g	0.3g
CALORIES	PROTEIN	FAT	SAT FAT	CARBS	SUGAR	FIBRE	SALT

ARTICHOKE TAGINE

Food snobs might shudder at the thought of buying ready-roasted artichoke hearts, but, if you have ever tried finding those pesky hearts in the middle of artichokes, you will be thanking me for this shortcut.

WHERE ON EARTH: char-grilled artichokes can be found in the 'refrigerated' section.

GLUTEN-FREE OPTION: use GF stock.

---

2 tablespoons **rapeseed oil**

2 **onions**, sliced

3 cloves **garlic**, chopped

1 teaspoon **turmeric**

1 teaspoon ground **ginger**

1 **veg stock cube**

1 ½ mugs/450ml **water**

2 **preserved lemons**, chopped

3 medium **sweet potatoes**, peeled and chopped into 2cm chunks

2 x 180g pack **char-grilled artichokes**, sliced

1 mug/180g **frozen peas**, defrosted

20 **black olives**, halved

1 **cauliflower**

2 tablespoons **rapeseed oil**

coriander to serve

1 Heat the oil in a large frying pan, or wok. Add the onions and garlic and fry until the onions begin to soften. Season well with salt and pepper.

2 Add the turmeric and ginger and stir.

3 Add the stock cube and water and bring to the boil.

4 Add the lemons, sweet potatoes, artichokes, peas and olives. Bring to the boil and then turn down to simmer, with a lid on the pan, for 10 minutes, or until the potato is tender.

5 Meanwhile, cut the cauliflower into florets and put into a food processor. Blitz until it looks like breadcrumbs.

6 Heat the oil in a large frying pan and add the cauliflower. Heat, stirring frequently, until the cauliflower begins to steam. Take off the heat.

7 Sprinkle the coriander over the tagine and serve with the cauliflower.

RDA 100%

575kcal	14g	26g	3g	64g	22g	19g	3g
CALORIES	PROTEIN	FAT	SAT FAT	CARBS	SUGAR	FIBRE	SALT

FARMER'S PIE

A good hearty winter-warmer. An interesting take on an old classic.

GLUTEN-FREE OPTION: use GF flour and stock.

---

2 **sweet potatoes**, peeled and cut into 1–2cm chunks

3 **potatoes**, peeled and cut into 1–2cm chunks

1 tablespoon **cashew cream**, see p207

BASE

2 tablespoons **rapeseed oil**

1 **onion**, chopped

2 cloves **garlic**, chopped

2 **carrots**, diced

250g **mushrooms**, chopped

leaves from 2 sprigs of **rosemary**, chopped

1 tablespoon **flour**

1 ½ mugs/450ml **water**

1 **veg stock cube**

1 tablespoon **coconut sugar**

2 x 400g tin **brown lentils**

2 tablespoons **tomato purée**

1 Preheat the oven to 180°C fan oven/200°C/gas 6.

2 Put the potatoes in a pan of boiling, salted water. Simmer for 6–8 minutes. Drain and return to the pan. Add the cashew cream and mash. Season well with salt and pepper.

3 Heat the oil in a large frying pan and fry the onions, garlic and carrots for 2 minutes.

4 Add the mushrooms and rosemary and fry for 1 minute.

5 Add the flour and stir.

6 Add the water and stock cube and bring to the boil. Add the rest of the ingredients and season well with salt and pepper.

7 Pour into a casserole dish. Pile the potatoes evenly over the top.

8 Bake in the oven for 25 minutes; the top should brown lightly.

RDA 100%

434kcal	12g	13g	2g	60g	20g	13g	1g
CALORIES	PROTEIN	FAT	SAT FAT	CARBS	SUGAR	FIBRE	SALT

CHESTNUT WELLINGTON

WHERE ON EARTH: whole, cooked chestnuts are often with the nuts, or the stuffing.

GLUTEN-FREE OPTION: use GF pastry, bread, and soy sauce.

4 **portobello mushrooms**

1 tablespoon **olive oil**

1 clove **garlic**, sliced

FILLING

2 tablespoons **milled flax seeds** + 6 tablespoons cold **water**

1 **onion**, cut into quarters

1 tablespoon chopped **rosemary**

2 cloves **garlic**, chopped

1 slice **bread**

200g **whole, cooked chestnuts**

100g **pecan nuts**

2 tablespoons **soy sauce**

2 x 280g sheets **vegan puff pastry**

soy cream to brush

200g **kale**

1 Preheat the oven to 180°C fan oven/200°C/gas 6.

2 Remove the stalks from the portobello mushrooms. Put the mushrooms on a baking tray and drizzle with oil. Sprinkle over the garlic and season well with salt and pepper. Roast in the oven for 15 minutes.

3 Meanwhile, prepare the Wellington filling. Put the flax seeds in a small bowl, with the water, and leave to stand for 10 minutes.

4 Put the onion, rosemary and garlic in a food processor and blitz until you have something resembling breadcrumbs. Add the bread and blitz.

5 Add the rest of the filling ingredients, including the flax seed, season and pulse a few times to mix.

6 Spread out one sheet of the pastry on a lined roasting tray. Put the portobello mushrooms in the centre and then pile in the chestnut mixture. Put the other sheet of pastry on top, wetting the edges with water to enable them to stick together. Trim the edges and pinch together.

7 Brush the top with the soy cream and bake in the oven for 40 minutes.

8 Meanwhile, put the kale on to simmer for 5 minutes.

RDA 100%

726kcal	13g	43g	12g	65g	9g	12g	2g
CALORIES	PROTEIN	FAT	SAT FAT	CARBS	SUGAR	FIBRE	SALT

CHESTNUT GRATIN

One of the major challenges with this recipe is getting it in the oven. The temptation to makes patterns over and over is very real. We settled on spiral here, but 'criss cross' is a classic choice too! Once cooked, another challenge is to get any 'seconds' at all.

WHERE ON EARTH: whole, cooked chestnuts are often with the nuts, or the stuffing.

GLUTEN-FREE OPTION: use GF stock.

---

4 medium **sweet potatoes**, peeled and cut into 3cm chunks

2 tablespoons **soy cream**

2 tablespoons **olive oil**

1 **onion**, sliced

2 cloves **garlic**, chopped

4 sticks **celery**, chopped

400g **whole, cooked chestnuts**, chopped

1 mug/300ml **soy cream**

2 tablespoons **nutritional yeast**

1 **veg stock cube**

200g **cavolo nero**

1 Preheat the oven to 180°C fan oven/200°C/gas 6. Grease a casserole dish.

2 Put the sweet potatoes in a saucepan of boiling, salted water. Simmer for 8 minutes. Drain and mash with the 2 tablespoons of soy cream.

3 Heat the oil in a large frying pan and add the onions, garlic and celery. Fry until the onion softens.

4 Add the chestnuts, 300ml of soy cream, nutritional yeast and stock cube. Season with salt and pepper. Bring to the boil and pour into the casserole dish.

5 Spread the mashed potato over the top. If you have any soy cream leftover, brush some on the top of the potatoes.

6 Bake in the oven for 25 minutes.

7 5 minutes before the end of the cooking time, put the cavolo nero in a pan of boiling, salted water and simmer for 3 minutes. Drain and serve.

RDA 100%

646kcal	14g	19g	3g	98g	29g	15g	0.5g
CALORIES	PROTEIN	FAT	SAT FAT	CARBS	SUGAR	FIBRE	SALT

LASAGNA

GLUTEN-FREE OPTION: make sure the lasagna sheets and stock are GF.

2 tablespoons **olive oil**

500g **chestnut mushrooms**, chopped

1 **onion**, chopped

2 cloves **garlic**, chopped

6 **tomatoes**, chopped

3 tablespoons **sun-dried tomato purée**

1 **veg stock cube**

2 tablespoons, freshly chopped **basil**

WHITE SAUCE

4 tablespoons **cornflour**

2 mugs/600ml **almond milk**

200g **vegan cream cheese**

3 tablespoons **cashew cream**, see p207

¼ teaspoon **nutmeg**

2 tablespoons **nutritional yeast**

300g **lasagna sheets**

2 **tomatoes**, sliced thinly

olive oil

1 Preheat the oven to 180°C fan oven/200°C/gas 6.

2 Heat the oil in a large frying pan, or wok. Add the mushrooms, onion and garlic and fry for 3–4 minutes.

3 Add the tomatoes, tomato purée and stock cube and bring to the boil. Season with salt and pepper. Take off the heat and stir in the basil.

4 To make the white sauce, put the ingredients in a saucepan and bring to the boil, stirring well as the sauce heats. Once boiling, take off the heat and season with salt and pepper.

5 Put a layer of the mushroom mixture in the bottom of the casserole dish, then a layer of lasagna sheets, then a layer of white sauce and then another layer of lasagna sheets. Repeat the process once more, finishing with the white sauce.

6 Arrange the sliced tomatoes over the top, season well and drizzle the oil over the top.

7 Bake in the oven for 45 minutes. The top should be nicely browned.

RDA 100%

| 799kcal | 25g | 44g | 15g | 79g | 14g | 8g | 2g |
| CALORIES | PROTEIN | FAT | SAT FAT | CARBS | SUGAR | FIBRE | SALT |

BAKED CAULIFLOWER

Roasting cauliflower is a great alternative to the classic 'boiling' technique. This is also a good 'prep-and-throw-in-the-oven' recipe.

6 **tomatoes**, halved

1 **onion**

1 clove **garlic**

2 tablespoons freshly chopped **parsley**

2 teaspoons **cumin seeds**

2 tablespoons **tomato purée**

1 tablespoon **cornflour**

1 **cauliflower**, cut into florets and then halved

zest and juice of a **lemon**

3 tablespoons **olive oil**

5 medium **potatoes**, cut into 2cm chunks

2 tablespoons **olive oil**

200g **chard**

1 Preheat the oven to 180°C fan oven/200°C/gas 6.

2 Put the tomatoes, onion, garlic and parsley in a food processor and blitz, leaving the mixture a little lumpy. Add the cumin seeds, tomato purée and cornflour. Season well with salt and pepper and pulse a couple of times. Pour into a casserole dish.

3 Put the cauliflower pieces on top of the tomato sauce.

4 Mix together the lemon zest, juice and the oil and pour that over the cauliflower. Season with salt and pepper.

5 Cover with foil and roast in the oven for 20 minutes. After 20 minutes take off the foil, and roast for a further 45 minutes.

6 Put the potatoes on a roasting tray, drizzle with the oil, season well with salt and pepper and mix everything together. Spread out on the tray and roast in the oven for 45 minutes.

7 Five minutes before the end of the cooking time, heat a little oil in a large frying pan. Add the chard and cook for 2 minutes, with a lid on the pan.

8 Serve together with the cauliflower and potatoes.

RDA 100%

383kcal	8g	18g	3g	43g	13g	7g	0.4g
CALORIES	PROTEIN	FAT	SAT FAT	CARBS	SUGAR	FIBRE	SALT

SWEET

£0.69 /PERSON | SERVES 12 | EASE ★★★★☆ | PREP 20 MINS | COOK 35 MINS | GF OPTION

PEANUT CHOCOLATE CAKE

WHERE ON EARTH: flaxseeds can be found in the 'Baking' section.

GLUTEN-FREE OPTION: use GF self-raising flour and add 1 teaspoon of xanthan gum.

CAKE

2 tablespoons **ground flaxseeds**

6 tablespoons **water**

100g **vegan margarine (Tomor)**

270g **coconut sugar**

130g **peanut butter**, see p211

1 teaspoon **vanilla extract**

300g **self-raising flour**

50g **cacao powder**

90ml **water**

230ml **almond milk**

TOPPING

150g **cashew cream**, see p207

3 tablespoons **cacao powder**

4 tablespoons **maple syrup**

100g **vegan margarine (Tomor)**

1 Preheat the oven to 170°C fan oven/190°C/gas 5. Line two 20cm cake tins.

2 Put the flaxseeds in a small bowl and add the first amount of water. Leave to stand for 10 minutes.

3 Put the margarine and coconut sugar in a bowl and beat well. Add the flaxseed mixture and beat well.

4 Add the rest of the cake ingredients and gently mix.

5 Divide between the cake tins and spread out evenly.

6 Bake in the oven for 30–35 minutes. The cake should 'bounce back' when lightly pressed.

7 Once the cakes are cooled, beat together the topping ingredients until light and fluffy. Sandwich the cakes together with some of the mixture and spread the rest over the top.

RDA 100%

510kcal	10g	29g	9g	53g	26g	4g	0.5g
CALORIES	PROTEIN	FAT	SAT FAT	CARBS	SUGAR	FIBRE	SALT

FRUIT AND NUT LOAF

WHERE ON EARTH: milled flaxseeds can be found in the 'Baking' section.

GLUTEN-FREE OPTION: use GF baking powder, GF plain flour and add 1 teaspoon xanthan gum with the flour.

1 tablespoon **milled flaxseeds**

3 tablespoons **cold water**

60g **medjool dates**, stoned and chopped

60g **ready-to-eat apricots**, chopped

50g **cranberries**

50g **raisins**

1 mug/300ml **strong, hot tea**

3 tablespoons **maple syrup**

zest of an **orange**

65g **vegan margarine (Tomor) melted**

200g **plain flour**

1 teaspoon **bicarbonate of soda**

1 teaspoon **baking powder**

1 teaspoon **mixed spice**

100g **cashews**, chopped

100g **pistachios**, chopped

1 Preheat the oven to 160°C fan oven/180°C/gas 4. Grease and line a loaf tin.

2 Put the flaxseeds in a small bowl and add the water. Leave to stand for 10 minutes.

3 Mix together the dates, apricots, cranberries, raisins, tea, maple syrup, zest of the orange and margarine in a bowl.

4 In a separate bowl, mix together the rest of the ingredients.

5 Add the wet ingredients to the bowl, along with the flaxseeds, and gently mix.

6 Pour into the prepared loaf tin and spread out evenly.

7 Bake in the oven for 45 minutes. Leave to cool and then slice.

RDA 100%

| 249kcal CALORIES | 5g PROTEIN | 13g FAT | 3g SAT FAT | 27g CARBS | 9g SUGAR | 5g FIBRE | 1g SALT |

£0.62 /PERSON · SERVES 12 · EASE ★★☆☆☆ · PREP 20 MINS · COOK 30 MINS · GF OPTION

BROWNIES

WHERE ON EARTH: flaxseeds can be found in the 'Baking' section.

GLUTEN-FREE OPTION: use GF self-raising flour and add 1 teaspoon xanthan gum.

1 tablespoon **flaxseeds**

3 tablespoons **cold water**

200g **100% cocoa solids chocolate**, see p215

250g **self-raising flour**

½ mug/100g **macadamias**, roughly chopped

2 tablespoons **cacao powder**

240g **dark brown sugar**

½ mug/150ml **rapeseed oil**

⅓ mug/100ml **almond milk**

1 Preheat the oven to 160°C fan oven/180°C/gas 4. Line and grease a traybake tin.

2 Put the flaxseeds in a small bowl, add the water and leave to stand for 10 minutes.

3 Put the chocolate in a small bowl over a pan of simmering water, and gently heat until melted.

4 Put the flour, macadamias, cacao powder and sugar in a large bowl. Mix together.

5 Add the flaxseeds, oil, milk and melted chocolate. Gently fold in and then pour into the prepared tin. Smooth out evenly.

6 Bake in the oven for 30 minutes.

RDA 100%

345kcal CALORIES | 4g PROTEIN | 25g FAT | 15g SAT FAT | 38g CARBS | 20g SUGAR | 2g FIBRE | 0.2g SALT

CHOCOLATE CRATER COOKIES

Pushing the chocolate into the centre of the cookies stops it from flowing all over the place. We tried a few other ways to solve this problem, it was very tiresome having to make these cookies over and over again!

GLUTEN-FREE OPTION: use GF self-raising flour + 1 teaspoon of xanthan gum.

---

1 tablespoon **flaxseeds**

3 tablespoons **water**

115g **vegan margarine (Tomor)**

200g **dark brown sugar**

1 teaspoon **vanilla extract**

140g **self-raising flour**

55g **cacao powder**

1 tablespoon **almond milk**

50g **100% cocoa solids chocolate**, see p215, chopped

1 Preheat the oven to 170°C fan oven/190°C/gas 5. Grease and line a large baking tray.

2 Put the flaxseeds in a small bowl and add the water. Leave to stand for 10 minutes.

3 Beat together the margarine, sugar and vanilla.

4 Stir in the flaxseeds mixture.

5 Add the flour, cacao powder, almond milk and mix together.

6 Form the mixture into 16 balls and place well apart on the baking tray. Push small piles of the chopped chocolate into the centre of the cookies.

7 Bake in the oven for 12 minutes.

RDA 100%

151kcal	2g	9g	4g	20g	12g	1g	0.2g
CALORIES	PROTEIN	FAT	SAT FAT	CARBS	SUGAR	FIBRE	SALT

ALMOND AND PISTACHIO COOKIES

WHERE ON EARTH: Flaxseeds can be found in the 'Baking' section.

GLUTEN-FREE OPTION: use GF self-raising flour and add 1 teaspoon xanthan gum.

---

1 tablespoon **milled flaxseeds**

3 tablespoons cold **water**

100g **vegan margarine (Tomor)**, softened

100g **light brown sugar**

100g **ground almonds**

1/2 teaspoon **vanilla extract**

120g **self-raising flour**

50g **pistachios**, chopped

1 Preheat the oven to 160°C fan oven/180°C/gas 4. Line 2 baking trays.

2 Put the flaxseeds in a small bowl and add the water. Leave to stand for 10 minutes.

3 Beat together the margarine and sugar.

4 Add the ground almonds and vanilla and beat into the mixture.

5 Stir in the flour and pistachios.

6 Roll into about 16 small balls. Place on the baking sheets and press down lightly with a fork.

7 Bake in the oven for 12 minutes.

RDA 100%

180

159kcal	3g	10g	3g	13g	7g	2g	0.5g
CALORIES	PROTEIN	FAT	SAT FAT	CARBS	SUGAR	FIBRE	SALT

BANANA CHOCOLATE MUFFINS

WHERE ON EARTH: Flaxseeds can be found in the 'Baking' section.

GLUTEN-FREE OPTION: use GF self-raising flour and add 1 teaspoon xanthan gum.

2 tablespoons **flaxseeds**

6 tablespoons **water**

300g **self-raising flour**

1 tablespoon **cacao powder**

1 teaspoon **baking powder**

1/2 teaspoon **bicarbonate of soda**

2 teaspoons **cinnamon**

175g **soft brown sugar**

100g **vegan margarine (Tomor)**, melted

200ml **almond milk**

3 **bananas**, mashed

50g **100% cocoa solids chocolate**, chopped, see p215

zest of an **orange**

1 Preheat the oven to 180°C fan oven/200°C/gas 6.

2 Put the flaxseeds and water in a small bowl and leave to stand for 10 minutes.

3 Mix the dry ingredients together in a large bowl.

4 Mix together the rest of the ingredients and add them to the dry ingredients, together with the flaxseed mixture.

5 Divide between 12 large muffin cases. Bake in the oven for 25–30 minutes.

RDA 100%

236kcal	3g	12g	5g	42g	20g	1g	0.3g
CALORIES	PROTEIN	FAT	SAT FAT	CARBS	SUGAR	FIBRE	SALT

£ 0.17 /PERSON — SERVES 12 — EASE ★★★☆☆ — PREP 20 MINS — COOK 20 MINS — GF OPTION

LEMON DRIZZLE CUP CAKES

GLUTEN-FREE OPTION: use GF baking powder, GF self-raising flour and add 1 teaspoon of xanthan gum.

200ml **soy milk**

4 teaspoons **cider vinegar**

200g **soft brown sugar**

230g **self-raising flour**

¼ teaspoon **bicarbonate of soda**

¼ teaspoon **baking powder**

80ml **rapeseed oil**

zest of a **lemon**

juice of ½ a **lemon**

2 tablespoons **soft brown sugar**

1 Put the soy milk in a bowl, with the cider vinegar, and leave to stand for 10 minutes.

2 Preheat the oven to 160°C fan oven/180°/gas 4. Prepare 12 bun cases.

3 Mix together the dry ingredients in a large mixing bowl.

4 Add the rapeseed oil and the lemon zest to the soy milk and add it all to the dry ingredients. Fold in gently, but as quick as you can, as the raising agents will begin to work straight away.

5 Divide between the bun cases and bake in the oven for 20 minutes. Leave to cool.

6 Once cooled, mix the lemon juice and sugar and drizzle over the cakes.

RDA 100%

| 205kcal | 2g | 7g | 0.5g | 35g | 19g | 0.2g | 0.2g |
| CALORIES | PROTEIN | FAT | SAT FAT | CARBS | SUGAR | FIBRE | SALT |

FLAP JACKS

Crunchy, crisp snacks, just don't eat too many at once.

GLUTEN-FREE OPTION: use GF oats.

125g **vegan margarine (Tomor)**

4 tablespoons **maple syrup**

²/₃ mug/100g **dark brown sugar**

2 mugs/200g **oats**

1 teaspoon **cinnamon**

1 teaspoon **ground ginger**

1 Preheat the oven to 170°C fan oven/190°C/gas 5. Line a traybake tin.

2 Put the margarine, maple syrup and sugar in a small pan and gently heat until the sugar is melted.

3 Put the oats and spices in a large bowl. Add the margarine mixture and stir well.

4 Pour into the traybake tin and even out.

5 Bake in the oven for 18 minutes.

6 Leave to cool before cutting into pieces.

RDA 100%

136kcal	1g	7g	3g	13g	8g	1g	0.1g
CALORIES	PROTEIN	FAT	SAT FAT	CARBS	SUGAR	FIBRE	SALT

CHOCOLATE ENERGY BARS

A single bar gives an injection of energy and protein. Ideal for keeping you going.

GLUTEN-FREE OPTION: use GF oats.

100g **100% cocoa solids chocolate**, see p215

150ml **water**

100ml **maple syrup**

4 tablespoons **peanut butter**, see p211

75g **pistachios**, roughly chopped

50g **pumpkin seeds**

50g **sunflower seeds**

100g **ready-to-eat dried apricots**, chopped

160g/8 **medjool dates**, stoned and chopped

250g **oats**

1 Preheat the oven to 160°C fan oven/180°C/gas 4. Grease and line a 20 x 20cm baking tray.

2 Put the chocolate, water, maple syrup and peanut butter in a saucepan and heat gently until everything is combined.

3 Mix the rest of the ingredients in a mixing bowl. Add the chocolate mixture and combine.

4 Press the mixture into the lined tin.

5 Bake in the oven for 15 minutes.

6 Leave to cool before cutting into slices.

RDA 100%

331kcal	10g	19g	6g	33g	20g	10g	1g
CALORIES	PROTEIN	FAT	SAT FAT	CARBS	SUGAR	FIBRE	SALT

ALMOND ENERGY BARS

A great pre- or post- workout snack that doesn't break the bank, at only 80p each!

GLUTEN-FREE OPTION: use GF oats.

200g **almond butter**, see p211

⅓ mug/100ml **maple syrup**

1 mug/150g **cashews**, roughly chopped

1 mug/100g **oats**

2 tablespoons **milled flaxseeds**

100g **ready-to-eat apricots**, chopped

1 Grease and line a 20 x 20cm cake tin.

2 Put the almond butter and maple syrup in a large saucepan and gently melt.

3 Stir in the rest of the ingredients and then press into the cake tin.

4 Leave in the fridge for 2 hours. Cut into bars.

RDA 100%

400kcal	12g	25g	2g	24g	13g	4.5g	0.1g
CALORIES	PROTEIN	FAT	SAT FAT	CARBS	SUGAR	FIBRE	SALT

STRAWBERRY ICE CREAM WITH SESAME BRITTLE

If you make this on a hot summer day, as we did, you will need to put the ice cream back in the freezer for ½ an hour to set a little more.

SESAME BRITTLE

100g **caster sugar**

1 tablespoon **sesame seeds**

ICE CREAM

500g **strawberries**, frozen

4 tablespoons **maple syrup**

250ml **soy yoghurt**

1 tablespoon **cashew cream**, see p207

1 Put the sugar in a clean frying pan and gently heat. Do not stir, but allow the sugar to melt and go lightly, golden brown.

2 Sprinkle over the sesame seeds and quickly pour out onto a baking sheet. Allow the mixture to spread as much as possible. Leave to cool and then gently knock with a knife handle to break into shards.

3 Put the ice cream ingredients in the food processor and blitz until the mixture is smooth. You can leave a few lumps of the strawberries if you wish.

4 Serve straight away with the brittle.

RDA 100%

284kcal	6g	8g	1g	46g	41g	2g	0.2g
CALORIES	PROTEIN	FAT	SAT FAT	CARBS	SUGAR	FIBRE	SALT

£ 1.50 /PERSON | SERVES 4 | EASE ★★★★☆ | PREP 30 MINS | COOK 18 MINS | GF OPTION

RASPBERRY FOOL AND SHORTBREAD

GLUTEN-FREE OPTION: use GF plain flour + 1 teaspoon xanthan gum in the shortbread.

SHORTBREAD

100g **caster sugar**

80g **Trex**

80g **vegan margarine (Tomor)**

205g **plain flour**

55g **cornflour**

CUSTARD

200ml **soy cream**

1 mug/300ml **soy milk**

small pinch of **turmeric** (optional for colour)

2 tablespoons **maple syrup**

2 tablespoons **cornflour**

1 teaspoon **vanilla bean paste**

400g **raspberries**

1 Preheat the oven to 160°C fan oven/180°C/gas 4.

2 Beat together the sugar, Trex and margarine. Add the flours and form into a dough.

3 Roll out and cut into shapes. Place on a baking sheet and bake in the oven for 18 minutes.

4 Put the custard ingredients in a small pan and whisk together. Bring to the boil, stirring occasionally. The custard should thicken. Leave to cool.

5 Put half the raspberries in a blender and blitz until smooth.

6 Layer in small bowls, with the other half of the raspberries on top. Serve with a few of the shortbreads per person.

RDA 100%

| 767kcal CALORIES | 7g PROTEIN | 43g FAT | 15g SAT FAT | 82g CARBS | 39g SUGAR | 4g FIBRE | 1g SALT |

APPLE CRUMBLE

GLUTEN-FREE OPTION: use GF oats.

WHERE ON EARTH: coconut chips can be found with nuts and dried fruit, or online. We buy ours in bulk from Healthy Supplies.

4 **Bramley apples**, peeled, cored and cut into 2cm chunks

2 tablespoons **coconut sugar**

1 tablespoon freshly grated **ginger**

½ teaspoon **cinnamon**

TOPPING

65g **coconut sugar**

95g **vegan margarine (Tomor)**

120g **oats**

50g **coconut chips**

65g **flaked almonds**

CUSTARD

400ml **almond milk**

2 tablespoons **cornflour**

2 tablespoons **maple syrup**

½ teaspoon **vanilla extract**

200ml **soy cream**

pinch **saffron**

1 Preheat the oven to 180°C fan oven/200°C/gas 6. Grease a pie dish.

2 Put the apples in a small pan with ½ mug water. Simmer until the apples begin to fall apart. Add the sugar, ginger and cinnamon. Pour into the prepared pie dish (or into 4 individual dishes).

3 For the topping, put the coconut sugar and margarine in a small pan and heat until the sugar dissolves. Add the oats, coconut chips and almonds and stir.

4 Pile on top of the apple mixture and press down lightly.

5 Bake in the oven for 25 minutes.

6 5 minutes before the end of the cooking time, make the custard. Take 2 tablespoons of the almond milk and mix with the cornflour, maple syrup and vanilla extract.

7 Put the rest of the milk, soy cream and saffron in a small pan. Bring to the boil and then pour over the cornflour mix. Stir well. Heat until it thickens.

8 Serve with the crumble.

RDA 100%

763kcal	11g	48g	18g	61g	47g	9g	1g
CALORIES	PROTEIN	FAT	SAT FAT	CARBS	SUGAR	FIBRE	SALT

CHOCOLATE MOUSSE

The great news about this recipe is that it makes enough for 5 people! That means you can hide one for later if there are just four of you.

150g **100% cocoa solids chocolate**, see p215

2 **avocados**, peeled and stoned

100ml **coconut cream**

150ml **maple syrup**

150ml **vegan yoghurt**

300g **strawberries**

1 Melt the chocolate in a bowl over a pan of simmering water.

2 Put the avocados and coconut cream in a food processor and blitz until smooth.

3 Add the maple syrup and chocolate and pulse a few times.

4 Divide between the bowls. Leave in the fridge for 1 hour to set.

5 Add a dollop of yoghurt and then a few strawberries to each bowl.

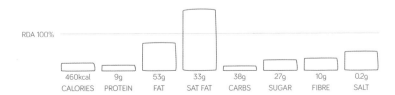

RDA 100%

| 460kcal | 9g | 53g | 33g | 38g | 27g | 10g | 0.2g |
| CALORIES | PROTEIN | FAT | SAT FAT | CARBS | SUGAR | FIBRE | SALT |

£ 2.13 /PERSON · SERVES 4-5 · EASE ★★★★☆ · PREP 30 MINS · GF

AVOCADO CHEESECAKE

This does not have your normal biscuit base, instead we have gone with almonds, cashews and dates. The avocado topping is unusually delicious.

BASE

75g **blanched almonds**

50g **cashews**

100g/5 **medjool dates**, stoned

30g **vegan margarine (Tomor)**, melted

1 tablespoon **cacao powder**

TOPPING

1 **avocado**

50ml **coconut cream**

200g **vegan cream cheese**

3 tablespoons **maple syrup**

juice of ½ **lemon**

300g **fresh mixed fruits**

1 Put the almonds and cashews in a food processor and blitz, leaving some chunks.

2 Add the medjool dates and pulse a few times.

3 Add the margarine and cacao powder and pulse a couple of times.

4 Put 2 dessertspoons of the mixture on each plate and squash lightly into a shape.

5 Put the topping ingredients in a food processor and blitz until smooth. Carefully, put tablespoons of the mixture on top of the bases on the plates.

6 Arrange the fruit on top and serve.

RDA 100%

| 631kcal | 11g | 47g | 23g | 37g | 27g | 8g | 1g |
| CALORIES | PROTEIN | FAT | SAT FAT | CARBS | SUGAR | FIBRE | SALT |

BROWNIE SUNDAE

Ben's daughter, Bella, was helping on this day. We asked her if she was going to eat anything savoury before she ate the brownies and she asked if strawberries counted as savoury!

CHOCOLATE SAUCE

100g **100% cocoa solids chocolate**, see p215

²/₃ mug/200ml **soy cream**

3 tablespoons **maple syrup**

400g **strawberries**

4 **brownies**, recipe p176

375g **vegan ice cream**

1 If you are making the brownies, make them now (see p176).

2 Put the chocolate sauce ingredients in a small pan and gently heat.

3 To make the strawberry sauce, put half of the strawberries in a blender and blitz until smooth.

4 Have fun assembling the components in whichever order you wish. Simply layer the sauces, ice cream and broken-up brownies.

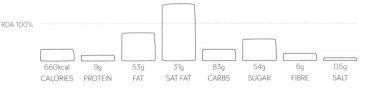

RDA 100%

| 660kcal | 9g | 53g | 31g | 83g | 54g | 6g | 0.5g |
| CALORIES | PROTEIN | FAT | SAT FAT | CARBS | SUGAR | FIBRE | SALT |

HOMEMADE

SWEET CHILLI SAUCE

A good one to keep in the fridge, it should keep for about a month. A great way to add an extra bite for those of you who like things a bit more spicy.

1 tablespoon **cornflour**

1 mug/300ml **water**

1 clove **garlic**, finely chopped

1 teaspoon **wine vinegar**

2 tablespoons **tomato purée**

2 tablespoons **maple syrup**

2 **fat red chillies**, chopped

1 Mix the cornflour and water together in a small saucepan. Add the rest of the ingredients.

2 Bring to the boil and simmer for one minute.

3 Store in a sterilised, airtight glass bottle, or jar (see p213), in the fridge.

 £3.52 /TOTAL   EASE ★☆☆☆☆   PREP 15 MINS   GF

NUT CREAM

Although this is simple, it does take some forethought to soak the nuts overnight before preparing it. Mainly used in sauces to give extra taste and adds loads of protein.

2 mugs/400g **nuts (cashews, or almonds)**

1 Put the nuts in a large bowl and pour over enough boiling water to cover them.

2 Leave to stand overnight.

3 Drain the nuts and place in a food processor. Blitz until smooth and store in a sterilised, airtight jar (see p213) in the fridge.

4 You can make this into soured cream by adding lemon juice, but only do this as you need it, as it will ferment.

BEETROOT PICKLE

You can add this pickle to top-off pretty much any dish and it will give it a new dimension. The sharpness can sometimes be a welcome addition to creamy dishes. Super-simple to make if you use the grater blade on a food processor.

3 large **raw beetroots**, peeled and cut into thin strips, or grated

2 tablespoons **cider vinegar**

1 tablespoon **coconut sugar**

1 Mix together and store in a sterilised, airtight jar (see p213) in the fridge.

TOMATO SAUCE

Another condiment that can be added to a variety of dishes, in place of the shop-bought version. Beware, this tomato sauce actually tastes like tomatoes!

2 tablespoons **olive oil**

1 **onion**, chopped

6 **tomatoes**, chopped

2 cloves **garlic**, chopped

2 tablespoons **tomato purée**

½ mug/150ml **water**

1 tablespoon **balsamic vinegar**

1 tablespoon **cornflour**

1 teaspoon **coconut sugar**

1 Heat the oil in a frying pan and add the onions. Fry until they begin to brown.

2 Add the tomatoes and garlic and continue to fry for 2 minutes.

3 Mix together the tomato purée, water, balsamic vinegar, cornflour and sugar. Add this to the pan and season well with salt and pepper. Bring to the boil and simmer for 2 minutes, stirring frequently.

4 Put in a blender and blitz until smooth.

5 Store in a sterilised, airtight glass bottle (see p213) in the fridge.

SAMBAL

A great way to add more spice to any 'Eastern' dish. It should keep in the fridge for a month.

WHERE ON EARTH: tamarind paste can be found with the spices.

---

4 **red onions**, cut into wedges

2 **red chillies**, deseeded

4 cloves **garlic**

2 teaspoons **turmeric**

4 tablespoons freshly grated **ginger**

4 teaspoons **tamarind paste**

3 tablespoons **coconut sugar**

1   Put everything in a food processor, or blender, and blitz until it forms a rough paste.

2   Heat a little oil in a frying pan and fry the paste for 2–3 minutes on a low heat.

3   Store in a sterilised, airtight jar (see p213) in the fridge.

NUT BUTTERS

We have used nut butter in quite a few recipes. It is easy to make if you have a food processor and is much healthier than most bought peanut butters. However, if you look carefully at the ingredients, you can find nut butters with no added sugar, or salt.

CASHEW NUT BUTTER
£3.95 /JAR

2 mugs/400g **cashews**

4 tablespoons **toasted sesame oil**

HAZELNUT BUTTER
£5.81 /JAR

2 mugs/400g **hazelnuts**

1 tablespoon **toasted sesame oil**

PEANUT BUTTER
£2.87 /JAR

2 mugs/400g **peanuts**

4 tablespoons **toasted sesame oil**

ALMOND BUTTER
£5.53 /JAR

2 mugs/400g **blanched almonds**

4 tablespoons **toasted sesame oil**

1 Put the nuts in a large frying pan and toast gently for 3–4 minutes. Keep them moving to avoid burning.

2 Place in a food processor and blitz for about 5 minutes, until they form a paste. Add the oil and blitz to form a soft paste.

3 Store in a sterilised, airtight jar (see p213).

COCONUT CRISPS

Sprinkle over meals to add a savoury crunch and a bit of saltiness. A simple 'beans on toast' is transformed with these crisps.

GLUTEN-FREE OPTION: use GF soy sauce.

4 tablespoons **soy sauce**

2 tablespoons **maple syrup**

1 teaspoon **paprika**

3 mugs/150g **coconut chips**

1. Preheat the oven to 170°C fan oven 190°C/gas 7.

2. Mix everything together in a large bowl.

3. Spread the mixture out over a large, greased, baking tray.

4. Bake in the oven for 10 minutes. Take out of the oven and stir. Bake in the oven for a further 10 minutes.

5. Allow to cool and then store in sterilised, airtight jars (see p213).

MANGO CHUTNEY

This recipe makes three jars of mango chutney, which should last you a while. You will need to sterilise the jars. Wash the jars and put them in the oven for 15 minutes, at 140°C fan oven 120°C/gas 1, before you fill them with chutney.

1 tablespoon **rapeseed oil**

1 **onion**, chopped

2 cloves **garlic**, chopped

1 **fat red chilli**, chopped

2 tablespoons freshly grated **ginger**

250ml **cider vinegar**

200g **coconut sugar**

2 **mangoes**, peeled and chopped

1 teaspoon **cumin**

1 teaspoon **coriander**

1 Heat the oil in a small saucepan. Add the onions, garlic, chilli and ginger and fry until the onions begin to soften.

2 Add the rest of the ingredients and bring to the boil. Turn down to simmer for 1 ½ hours.

3 Store in the sterilised, airtight jar in the fridge.

SALSA VERDE

Store in the fridge. Quick and simple to make and a great addition, giving both flavour and colour to all sorts of dishes.

2 cloves **garlic**

25g fresh **parsley**

50g fresh **basil**

25g fresh **mint**

2 tablespoons **capers**

3 **pickled gherkins**

2 teaspoons **Dijon mustard**

3 tablespoons **wine vinegar**

8 tablespoons **extra virgin olive oil**

1 Put everything in a blender and blitz until smooth.

2 Store in a sterilised, airtight jar (see p213) in the fridge.

100% SUGAR-FREE DARK CHOCOLATE

Throughout this book we suggest using 100% cocoa solids chocolate, as it contains no processed sugar and no dairy. We understand it is expensive to buy, so for that reason, we make our own. We buy our ingredients from 'Healthysupplies.com'. Alternatively, you can buy high-percent, cocoa solids chocolate, if you are not fussy about being completely sugar-free.

COOKING CHOCOLATE

250g **cacao butter**

125g **cacao powder**

EATING CHOCOLATE

250g **cacao butter**

125g **cacao powder**

90ml **pure maple syrup**

1 teaspoon **sugar-free vanilla extract**

1 Simply melt the cacao butter in a small saucepan, being careful not to overheat. Take off the heat and add the cacao powder and whisk together until smooth.

2 If you are making 'eating' chocolate, add the maple syrup and vanilla and stir well.

3 Pour into either a silicon chocolate mold, or a plastic box, and leave to set. Keep stored in the fridge.

CHILLI JAM

Quick and easy to make, and as you can see, we have re-used some of our jars from other projects, so no need to buy anything fancy. Just make sure they are sterilised first (see p213).

1 tablespoon **rapeseed oil**

3 **fat red chillies**, chopped

2 tablespoons freshly grated **ginger**

½ mug/150ml **cider vinegar**

½ mug/150ml **water**

150g **coconut sugar**

2 tablespoons **cornflour**

2 tablespoons **water**

1   Heat the oil in a frying pan. Add the chillies and ginger and fry for 1 minute.

2   Add the cider vinegar, water and coconut sugar and simmer for 2 minutes.

3   Mix together the cornflour and water and add. Simmer for 2 minutes. Leave to cool slightly and then store in a sterilised, airtight jar (see p213) in the fridge.

HOT CHILLI SAUCE

Another good one to add more 'kick', if that is your preference.

1 tablespoon **rapeseed oil**

1 **red onion**, sliced

2 cloves **garlic**, chopped

2 **tomatoes**, chopped

3 **fat red chillies**, chopped

3 tablespoons **tomato purée**

1 teaspoon **cornflour** + 2 tablespoons **water**

1   Heat the oil in a saucepan. Add the onions and garlic and fry until the onions soften.

2   Add the tomatoes and chillies and fry for 1 minute.

3   Add the tomato purée. Mix the cornflour with the water and add. Bring to the boil. Season with salt and pepper.

4   Take off the heat and blitz.

5   Store in a sterilised, airtight jar (see p213) in the fridge.

ONION BHAJIS WITH RAITA

BATTER

1 tablespoon **flaxseeds**

3 tablespoons **water**

125ml **water**

150g **garam flour**

1 teaspoon **turmeric**

2 teaspoons **cumin**

2 teaspoons **paprika**

¼ teaspoon freshly ground **salt**

2 **red onions**, sliced

²/₃ mug/200ml **rapeseed oil**

RAITA

200g **soy yoghurt**

25g freshly chopped **coriander**

juice of a **lemon**

½ **cucumber**, grated

1 Put the flaxseeds with the water, in a small bowl and leave to stand for 10 minutes. Strain.

2 In a large bowl, beat together the rest of the batter ingredients, including the flaxseeds.

3 Mix the onions into the batter.

4 Heat the oil in a large frying pan. Try a little of the batter and if it sizzles, the oil is ready. Add small bundles of the onions; you will need to fry in batches. Fry on both sides until nicely browned. Take out and drain on some paper towel.

5 Mix together the raita ingredients and serve with the bhajis.

6 Perfect as an 'add-on' to a curry recipe.

INDEX

SIGN UP...

AT NOSHBOOKS.COM/VEGAN

TO GET NEW PLANT-BASED

RECIPES EMAILED TO YOU

Published by: Intrade (GB) Ltd
Contact: joymay@mac.com

ISBN: 978-0-9932609-7-1

Printed in China

1st Edition: March 2019

Author: Joy May

Design & Photography: Ben May & Tim May

Proof-reading: Fran Maciver

Editor: Ron May

Recipe prices are an average of
Tesco and Sainsbury's pricing
as at **September 2018.**

Thanks for your support:

HEALTHY SUPPLIES
THE HEALTH FOOD SPECIALISTS

KENWOOD